FOURTH EDITION

READY TO WRITE 3

FROM PARAGRAPH TO ESSAY

KAREN BLANCHARD • CHRISTINE ROOT

Ready to Write 3: From Paragraph to Essay
Fourth Edition

Pearson Education, 221 River Street, Hoboken, NJ 07030

Acknowledgments: We are grateful to several people whose contributions strengthened this book. Thank you to Kathy Buruca and Robby Steinberg for their inspired suggestions, Daniel Blanchard, Hasan Halkali, and Matthew Root for allowing us to use their essays, as well as Nonie Gadson and Erica Hirshler at the Museum of Fine Arts, Boston.

Staff credits: The people who made up the Ready to Write team, representing editorial, production, design, and manufacturing, are Pietro Alongi, Tracey Cataldo, Rosa Chapinal, Aerin Csigay, Mindy DePalma, Warren Fischbach, Pam Fishman, Leslie Johnson, Niki Lee, Amy McCormick, Robert Ruvo, and Kristina Skof.
Cover image: Evgeny Karandaev / Shutterstock
Text composition: ElectraGraphics, Inc.
Text font: Formata Light

Library of Congress Cataloging-in-Publication Data
A catalog record for the print edition is available from the Library of Congress.
ISBN-10: 0-13-439933-1   ISBN-13: 978-0-13-439933-1

Printed in the United States of America
31 2023

To the memory of Michael Blanchard:
For his love of good writing and his enduring spirit.

Contents

Scope and Sequence

Chapter	Writing Skills	Writing Tips	Writing Activities
PART 1: THE ELEMENTS OF GOOD WRITING			
1 **GETTING READY TO WRITE** **Learning Outcome:** Paragraph Writing: Write a paragraph using the steps of the writing process	• Identifying purpose: to entertain, to inform, to persuade • Narrowing a general topic • Recognizing and using the steps of the writing process • Practicing prewriting (brainstorming, clustering, listing)	• Using the acronym SPA (Subject, Purpose, Audience) • Brainstorming	• Writing a letter about borrowing money for two different audiences: a friend or a loan officer at a bank • Writing two paragraphs about the same subject, each with a different purpose and audience • Practicing prewriting techniques • Use the steps of the writing process to write a paragraph about travel
2 **WRITING PARAGRAPHS** **Learning Outcome:** Paragraph Writing: Write paragraphs using time order, spatial order, and order of importance.	• Understanding the Parts of a paragraph • Writing Topic Sentences • Understanding paragraph organization, unity, and support • Identifying irrelevant sentences • Using transition signals	• Paragraph Form • Topic Sentences • Using facts, reasons, and examples for support • Concluding Sentences • Paragraph titles • Synonyms	• Writing topic, supporting, and concluding sentences • Writing a paragraph about your favorite season, violence on TV, conserving energy • Writing paragraphs organized by time order, spatial order, and order of importance • Writing a paragraph describing how your bedroom reflects your personality • Writing a paragraph about planning a weekend trip to another city

3
REVISING AND EDITING
Learning Outcome:
Essay Writing: Use the writing process to write an essay about the pressures of being a student
	• Checking grammar for
	  • Agreement of subjects and verbs, pronouns and nouns, possessive pronouns and adjectives
	  • Sentence fragments
	  • Run-on sentences
	• Punctuation and capitalization
	  • Pronoun reference
	  • Subordinating Conjunctions
	  • Gerunds and Infinitives
	  • Parallel Structure
	  • Spelling Rules
	• Revise and improve writing by
	  • including a clear topic sentence, appropriate transitions, and enough supporting evidence
	  • eliminating irrelevant sentences
	  • adding new ideas
	  • rearranging sentences
		• Revising
		• Spelling
			• Using the writing process to write a travel article

Chapter	Writing Skills	Writing Tips	Writing Activities
4 **WRITING ESSAYS** **Learning Outcome:** Essay Writing: Write a five-paragraph essay about a preference such as living in a small town or living in a big city.	• Parts of an essay • Introductions • Thesis statements • Using revising checklist, editing checklist, peer revision worksheet • Using transitional signals for a summary or a conclusion	• Organizing essays • Introductions • Thesis Statements • Supporting Paragraphs	• Writing, revising, and editing an essay on the pressures of being a student • Writing a five-paragraph essay about a preference (e.g., living in a big city v. a small town)

PART 2: TYPES OF ESSAYS

Chapter	Writing Skills	Writing Tips	Writing Activities
5 **PROCESS ESSAYS** **Learning Outcome:** Essay Writing: Use the writing process to write a process essay using time order	• Process essay plan • Transition words for Process essays • Thesis statements for process essays	• Time Order • Audience	• Writing a one-paragraph description of the process • Writing, revising and editing a "how to" essay about • washing a car • making rice, tea, a salad, noodles, etc. • writing a good paragraph or essay • studying for an exam • annoying your teacher, your boss, or your parents • making a paper airplane, knitting a scarf, painting a picture, etc.
6 **DIVISION AND CLASSIFICATION ESSAYS** **Learning Outcome:** Essay Writing: Use the writing process to write a division and classification essay	• Division and classification essay plan • Dividing a topic into groups • The Language of Classification: Useful Sentence Patterns for Thesis Statements	• Grouping Ideas • Thesis Statements for Division and Classification Essays	• Using the writing process to write a division-classification essay about TV commercials • Using the writing process to write about • types of mistakes people make when learning a second language • types of students, athletes, etc • types of martial arts • kinds of bad habits • kinds of engineers (doctors, lawyers) • types of drivers, shoppers, etc • kinds of novels, movies, etc

Chapter	Writing Skills	Writing Tips	Writing Activities
7 **CAUSE AND EFFECT ESSAYS** **Learning Objective:** Essay Writing: Use the writing process to write a cause and effect essay	• Cause or effect essay plan • Using transition signals for cause or effect relationships • Sentence patterns for topic sentences and thesis statements for cause or effect paragraphs and essays	• Ordering Supporting Paragraphs	• Using the writing process to write a cause or effect essay about a topic, such as the explosion of the Internet • Using the writing process to write a cause/effect essay about the causes of heart disease • Using information online to write about the causes or effects of an important historical event
8 **COMPARISON AND CONTRAST ESSAYS** **Learning Objective:** Essay Writing: Use the writing process to write a comparison and contrast essay	• The Language of Comparison and Contrast: Useful Phrases and Sentence Patterns • The point-by-point method to organize paragraphs in comparison/ contrast essays • The block method to organize paragraphs in comparison/ contrast essays	• Choosing a topic • Point-by-point format • Block format	• Writing a comparison paragraph about the similarities of two twins • Writing a point-by-point comparison-contrast essay about two characters in a movie or book • Using the writing process to write an essay comparing and contrasting: • yourself and another member of your family. • an aspect of your culture, such as eating habits, education, government, economy, religion, or social life, with the same aspect of another culture. • a photo and a painting of the same scene. • Two people you have worked with, such as two coworkers at a job, two students in a group, or two bosses you have had.
9 **PROBLEM-SOLUTION ESSAYS** **Learning Objective:** Essay Writing: Use the writing process to write a problem and solution essay	• Developing problem-solution essays by using a step-by-step essay plan	• Using Transitions	• Using the writing process to write problem-solution essays about crime, etc. • Writing e-mails and letters for an Internet advice column • Using a peer revision worksheet, a revising checklist, and an editing checklist • Writing a paragraph about an everyday problem by finding a solution online • Writing a paragraph about an everyday problem by finding a solution online • Using the writing process to write a problem / solution about essay about: • overcrowding in your school • the generation gap • an argument with a friend • deforestation • access to the workplace for the disabled • drug abuse

Chapter	Writing Skills	Writing Tips	Writing Activities
PART 3: WRITING FOR SPECIFIC PURPOSES			
10 **WRITING SUMMARIES** **Learning Objective:** Paragraph Writing: Write a one-paragraph summary of an article	• Follow steps for writing summaries: • Revise draft of summary (check for accuracy, minor points, any of your own thoughts). • Edit for grammar, spelling, punctuation, and capitalization.	• Use your own words	• Using the writing process to write a one-paragraph summary of a magazine article
11 **EXPRESSING YOUR OPINIONS** **Learning Objective:** Essay Writing: Write a five-paragraph essay that expresses your opinion on a controversial topic	• Using revising and editing checklists	• Phrases that introduce opinions	• Using the writing process to write opinion paragraphs about two famous paintings, two poems, etc. • Using the writing process to write opinion essays about controversial issues • Writing a five-paragraph essay to express your opinion on a sample exam question
12 **WRITING UNDERGRADUATE AND GRADUATE SCHOOL APPLICATION ESSAYS** **Learning Objective** Essay Writing: Write an undergraduate or graduate application essay	• Pay attention to the principles of good writing. • Tips for writing application essays • Write an interesting introduction, body, and conclusion.	• Get Second Opinions	• Using the writing process to write an undergraduate application essay and a personal statement essay

Introduction

Ready to Write 3 is a writing skills text designed for intermediate and high-intermediate students who are ready to write more than paragraph-level pieces. It builds on the fundamentals that students learned in *Ready to Write 1* and *Ready to Write 2,* giving students the confidence they need to write longer pieces.

The *Ready to Write* series came about because of our threefold conviction that

- Students learn to write well and achieve a more complete English proficiency by learning and practicing writing skills simultaneously with other English language skills they are learning;

- students are interested in and capable of writing expressively in English on a variety of provocative and sophisticated topics if they are supplied with the organizational tools to do so;

- students need to be explicitly taught that different languages organize information differently, and they need to be shown how to organize information correctly in English.

Approach

Ready to Write 3 is based on the premise that because languages organize information differently, students need to be shown how to organize information in English if they are to write effective essays. Students also need to understand that good writing is not necessarily a natural gift. It involves complex skills that can be learned and mastered. The text fosters competency in all of these skills by leading students step-by-step through the writing process.

The activities in *Ready to Write 3* help students become competent, independent writers by engaging them in the process of writing and by encouraging them to explore and organize their ideas in writing. Students are called upon to write often and on a broad range of meaningful, thought-provoking topics. The tasks are presented in a clear, straightforward manner for ease of instruction. Incorporated into the tasks is a variety of follow-up personal- and peer-revision activities. Although *Ready to Write 3* is a writing book, students practice their reading, speaking, listening, and analytical skills as they progress through the text.

The Fourth Edition

While much has been updated and expanded in this Fourth Edition of *Ready to Write 3,* what has not changed is the successful, basic approach that has made the series so popular all these years.

Two popular features from previous editions—*You Be the Editor* and *On Your Own*—appear throughout *Ready to Write 3. You Be the Editor* provides effective practice in error correction and proofreading to help students monitor their own errors, especially those covered in Chapter 3, Revising and Editing. An answer key for these exercises appears at the end of the book. *On Your Own* provides students with further individual practice in the skills they have learned

This fourth edition of *Ready to Write 3* includes these important new and expanded features:

- learning outcomes at the beginning of each chapter focus students on the chapter's goals

- an engaging four-color design

- step-by-step activities that guide students from personal to academic writing
- expanded, targeted grammar practice in the context of writing
- updated examples, as well as model paragraphs and essays, that illustrate organizing elements such as topic sentences, supporting details, and signal words (for paragraphs), and thesis statements, introduction, body, and conclusion (for essays)
- instruction and practice that helps students progress from writing paragraphs to composing essays that require finding a focus, comparing and contrasting, describing, analyzing data, writing test answers, and summarizing
- coverage of all of the steps in the writing process: prewriting, writing, and revising and editing
- *Writing Tips* with stepped-out guidelines for writing
- peer revision worksheets
- web-based activities with more writing activities
- *Essential Online Resources* with answer keys, as well as additional grammar and writing activities.

Chapter Features

Learning Outcomes: Each chapter begins with objectives so students can see the intended goals of a chapter and what their learning experience will be. The learning outcomes are brief, written statements that help students see the knowledge, skills, and habits of work that they are expected to acquire by the end of the chapter. There are two learning outcomes: one for paragraph writing and one for life skills writing.

Grammar for Writing: Each chapter focuses on one or two specific grammar points along with helpful charts, clear explanations, and attendant practice. By practicing new grammar points in the context of their writing, students boost their writing accuracy and learn to vary their sentence types.

The Steps of the Writing Process: Each chapter provides guided instruction in the steps that are integral to good writing i.e. prewriting, writing, and revising. Revising checklists are provided for students to use to improve their paragraphs and write their final draft.

Writer's Tips: This feature provides helpful information on how to write and refine paragraphs. These tips include choosing a topic and working toward unity, accuracy and coherence.

On Your Own: Coming toward the end of most chapters, these activities provide students with yet another opportunity to write on a topic of their own choosing from among several suggested prompts. After they write a paragraph, students are instructed to use the revising checklist to improve their paragraphs, thereby practicing independent writing and revising.

You Be the Editor: This self-correcting exercise near the end of each chapter is intended to give students the opportunity to look for and correct the most common grammar mistakes made by intermediate and high-intermediate students as they learn to write in English. Each paragraph has a stated number of mistakes for students to look for. The answers for each chapter appear in the back of the book. Students can use the answers to check their own work and become independent and confident writers.

We hope that you and your students enjoy working through this text now that they are *ready to write* more.
—KLB and CBR

PART 1

THE ELEMENTS OF GOOD WRITING

Not everyone is a naturally gifted writer. Fortunately, writing is a skill that you can practice and master. In some ways, writing is like driving a car. If you have ever driven in another country, you know that some of the rules of the road may be different. Just as the rules for driving differ from country to country, the conventions for writing may change from language to language.

Writing in English involves more than mastering its vocabulary and grammar. Language, including written language, is a reflection of the thought patterns of native speakers. In order to write well in English, it is important to understand the way native speakers organize their thoughts. That is why it rarely works to write something in your native language and then translate it into English. The words may be in English, but the logic, organization, and thought patterns reflect those of your native language.

To write effectively in English, you need to conform to the accepted patterns of organization. Practicing these patterns will put you on the road to becoming a better writer.

LEARNING OUTCOME   **Paragraph Writing:** Write a paragraph identifying subject, purpose, and audience

Many students learning a new language think that writing is the most difficult skill to master. Putting your ideas down on paper may seem more complicated and frustrating than expressing them orally. In this chapter, you will learn some techniques to make your writing experience more successful.

DETERMINING YOUR ATTITUDE TOWARD WRITING

Your attitude toward anything that you do in life greatly affects your success in doing it. Writing is not an exception. Think about your attitude toward writing *in your native language* as you complete the following exercises.

A **Circle your responses to the following statements about writing in your own language.**

Use the following scale:

1 = Strongly Agree   2 = Agree   3 = Neutral
4 = Disagree   5 = Strongly Disagree

a. I enjoy keeping a diary. 1   2   3   4   5

b. I like to write letters to my family and friends. 1   2   3   4   5

c. Writing about my feelings helps me relax. 1   2   3   4   5

d. I enjoy working on reports for school and work. 1   2   3   4   5

e. I enjoy writing personal essays. 1   2   3   4   5

f. I like to write poems, stories, or songs. 1   2   3   4   5

g. I enjoy using email. 1   2   3   4   5

h. I like to write blogs. 1   2   3   4   5

i. Writing is a creative outlet for me. 1   2   3   4   5

j. I feel good about my writing ability. 1   2   3   4   5

Add the numbers of your answers and put the total in the box. ☐

B Take the number from the box on page 2 and divide it by ten. The final number is your average score for the ten questions. Overall, it will tell you how much you like to write. The closer your score is to "1," the more you like to write. The closer your score is to "5," the less you like to write.

C Based on your answers, what general conclusions can you make about your attitude toward writing in your native language?

_____

_____

_____

D Write a paragraph about your general attitude toward writing.

_____

_____

_____

_____

_____

_____

_____

WillWriteForChocolate.com   ©2007 Debbie Ridpath Ohi - Twitter: @inkyelbows

E In small groups, share your main ideas from the paragraph you wrote about your general attitude toward writing. Then discuss the following questions.

1. What kinds of things do you enjoy writing about?

2. What kinds of writing do you think will be required in university classes?

3. What types of writing does your job or future profession require?

4. What do you hope to gain from this course?

ELEMENTS OF GOOD WRITING: SPA

Good writers have to keep several things in mind as they write. Three of the most important things are *subject*, *purpose*, and *audience*.

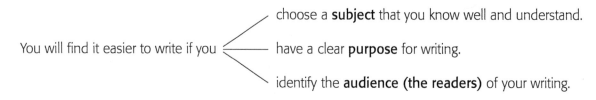

You will find it easier to write if you

choose a **subject** that you know well and understand.

have a clear **purpose** for writing.

identify the **audience (the readers)** of your writing.

WRITER'S TIP: Using the Acronym SPA

SPA is an acronym that stands for *subject, purpose*, and *audience*. SPA will help you remember these things.

Keeping these three things in mind will help your writing stay focused.

Subject (Ask yourself, "What am I going to write about?")

In order to write well, it is helpful to choose a subject that interests you and that you know and understand. If your teacher assigns a subject, try to find an angle or focus of that subject that you find interesting and want to explore.

It is important to choose a subject that is not too broad. You will usually have to go through a process of narrowing down the general subject until you find an appropriate topic.

Suppose *entertainment* is your general subject. *Entertainment* is too broad, so you need to narrow it down to a more focused topic. You could narrow it to a specific kind of entertainment, such as movies. Movies is still too general, however, so you need to do some further narrowing. Look at how one student narrowed down the general subject of entertainment to a specific topic.

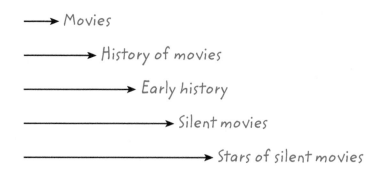

ENTERTAINMENT

→ Movies

→ History of movies

→ Early history

→ Silent movies

→ Stars of silent movies

Finding a Subject

Narrow down each of the following general subjects until you find a specific angle that you would be interested in writing about. Then write your narrowed topics on the board. Discuss and compare the various topics with your classmates.

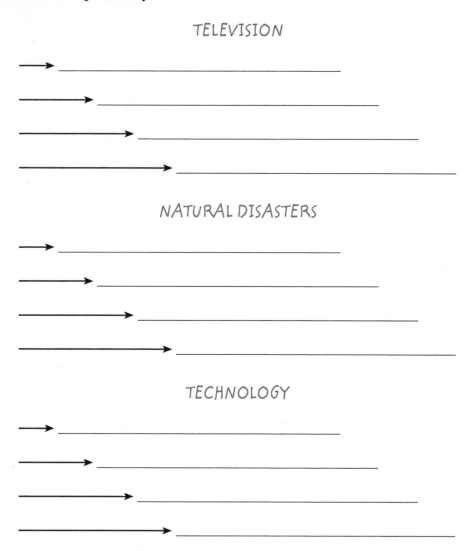

TELEVISION

⟶ _____

⟶ _____

⟶ _____

⟶ _____

NATURAL DISASTERS

⟶ _____

⟶ _____

⟶ _____

⟶ _____

TECHNOLOGY

⟶ _____

⟶ _____

⟶ _____

⟶ _____

Purpose (Ask yourself, "Why am I writing this?")

Whenever you write something, it is important to think about your purpose. The *purpose* is the reason you are writing.

The three most common purposes for writing are

- to entertain;
- to inform; and
- to persuade.

However, these three purposes are not always mutually exclusive. It is possible for a piece of writing to have several purposes at the same time. For example, an article may be amusing but also educational or persuasive.

Identifying Purpose

Identify the author's main purpose in each of these pieces of writing.

Avalanche

An **avalanche** is any fast movement of snow, ice, mud, or rock down a mountainside. Avalanches are natural forms of erosion and are often seasonal; they can reach speeds of more than 200 miles per hour. They are caused by events such as earthquake tremors, human-made disturbances, and excessive rainfall.

Destruction from avalanches results both from the avalanche wind (the air pushed ahead of the mass) and from the actual impact of the avalanche material.

1. _____

Dear Family and Friends,

I am writing to tell you about an exciting new adventure that I need your help with. As you know, I just graduated from culinary school. It has always been my dream to open my own restaurant. However, opening a restaurant is quite expensive, and I really need some financial assistance. Any amount of money you could offer would help me cover the high costs of opening a restaurant. For example, the money will help me pay rent for the restaurant, which is $6,000 per month. I will also use the money to buy restaurant equipment and furniture. In addition, the money will go toward the ingredients for the delicious meals I will cook, but I need some cash to cover the first few paychecks for my servers and kitchen staff. Your generosity would be very helpful, and I promise to pay you back as soon as the restaurant starts making money. I'm sure that I will have a successful new restaurant with your help. Remember, if you donate money, you will always eat for free!

Thanks,
Chef Dan

2. _____

Are you looking for a great travel destination?

If so, I suggest you head to Arizona.

With its much-loved past and modern amenities, you won't be disappointed. Explore Arizona's rich Native American history by taking a guided tour of the spectacular Monument Valley or visiting the Heard Museum in Phoenix. The deserts, rivers, mountains, and canyons of Arizona are spectacular. The Grand Canyon is truly one of the world's most amazing natural wonders. You won't want to miss the red rock country of Sedona for an experience of a lifetime. Take my advice and plan a trip to Arizona.

3. _____

> When I was a boy of fourteen, my father was so ignorant I could hardly stand to have the old man around. But when I got to be twenty-one, I was astonished by how much he'd learned in seven years.
> —Mark Twain

4. _____

http://Gloria_Estefan

Home | Article | Discussion | View Source | History

navigation
■ Main page
■ Contents
■ Featured content
■ Current events
■ Random article

interaction
■ About Us
■ Community porta
■ Recent changes
■ Contact Us
■ Help

Gloria Estefan

Gloria Estefan was one of the first Latin American artists to successfully incorporate Latin beats and sound with American pop music to produce hit songs across the United States. With her group, The Miami Sound Machine, Estefan began including Cuban sounds in her pop-inspired music early in the 1990s. She quickly gained recognition as a powerful Latin singer whose unique music won the hearts and ears of many American music lovers. Pioneering artists such as Gloria Estefan paved the way for the Latin superstars who followed. She helped tune the American ear to Latin music and continues to play an important role in the Latin pop scene.

5. _____

FOX UNIVERSITY

Since we are planning to do some renovations on the Fox Undergraduate Library this summer, the library hours for both summer sessions will be changed. The Fox building will be completely closed for the first summer session, and undergraduate students will be able to use all the facilities of the Graylord Graduate Library. The Graylord Library will be open seven days a week from 8 A.M. to 11 P.M. During the second summer session, the first floor of the Fox Library will be open from 9 A.M. to noon, Monday through Friday. All other floors will remain closed until the beginning of the fall semester in September. Again, undergraduate students enrolled in summer classes will have complete access to the Graylord facilities. We apologize for the inconvenience but look forward to better serving you with our upgraded and expanded undergraduate library next fall.

6. _____

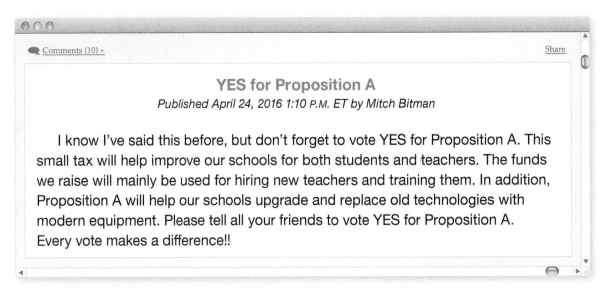

Comments (10) »   Share

YES for Proposition A
Published April 24, 2016 1:10 P.M. ET by Mitch Bitman

I know I've said this before, but don't forget to vote YES for Proposition A. This small tax will help improve our schools for both students and teachers. The funds we raise will mainly be used for hiring new teachers and training them. In addition, Proposition A will help our schools upgrade and replace old technologies with modern equipment. Please tell all your friends to vote YES for Proposition A. Every vote makes a difference!!

7. _____

Renting a car offers many attractive advantages to the traveler: independence, convenience, dependability—and a sudden, massive lowering of the IQ. I know what I'm talking about here. I live in Miami, and every winter we have a huge infestation of rental car drivers, who come down here seeking warm weather and the opportunity to make sudden left turns without signaling, across six lanes of traffic, into convenience stores. My wife and I have affectionately nicknamed these people "Alamos" because so many of them seem to get their cars from Alamo, which evidently requires that every driver leave several major brain lobes as a deposit. We're tempted to stay off the highways altogether during tourist season, just stockpile food, and spend the entire winter huddled in our bedrooms, but we're not sure we'd be safe there.

Dave Barry's Only Travel Guide You'll Ever Need, by Dave Barry

8. _____

B **Complete the chart. Put each type of writing in the correct box or boxes.**

TYPES OF WRITING		
advertisements	jokes	op-eds (opinions/editorials)
blogs	letters	poems
directions	memos	reports
emails	newspaper articles	stories
essays	novels	textbooks
restaurant reviews	song lyrics	recipes

ENTERTAIN	INFORM	PERSUADE

C Look through your local newspaper and find one example of writing that entertains, one that informs, and one that persuades. Bring your articles to class to share with your classmates.

1. Which kind of article (entertaining, informational, or persuasive) was the easiest to find?

   _____

   _____

2. Which kind was the most difficult to find? Why?

   _____

   _____

3. Which kind of writing do you think students are usually asked to do?

   _____

   _____

Audience (Ask yourself, "Who is going to read this?")

What you write about (subject) and your reason for writing (purpose) are greatly affected by whom you are writing for (audience). Because you will usually be writing for an audience, you will communicate your ideas more effectively if you keep that audience in mind. Remember that all audiences have expectations, but those expectations vary from one audience to another.

As you work through this book, your audience will usually be your teacher or classmates. However, occasionally you will be asked to write with another audience in mind. This will give you practice choosing the appropriate words and varying your tone.

PRACTICE **A** Read the following two emails and notice the difference in tones.

To: mysister@internet.net
From: yourbrother@internet.net
Subject: Mexico City

Hi,

Guess what? I'll be in Mexico City on the 8th for a business meeting. I'll have some free time in the P.M. Let's have dinner together, OK? By the way, I bumped into your old friend Sally last week. She asked me how you were doing. I guess she hasn't heard from you in a while. Why don't you give her a call?
See you soon.

Jack

To: mrhill@internet.net
From: jnorris@internet.net
Subject: Seoul

Dear Mr. Hill:

I will be in Seoul on October 8th and would like to meet with you and show you our new product line. If this is agreeable to you, I can meet you at your office at 4 P.M. I look forward to hearing from you.

Jack Norris

B In small groups, make a list of the differences between the two emails. Which one uses more formal language? Which one is more conversational?

1. _____

2. _____

3. _____

4. _____

Writing for Different Audiences

A letter you write to your best friend asking him or her to lend you some money is quite different from a letter to a bank loan officer. The two letters probably would include different expressions and have different tones.

A On a piece of paper, write a letter to your best friend asking to borrow money.

B On another piece of paper, write a letter to the loan officer at a bank asking to borrow money.

C Compare your two letters and answer the following questions.

1. Which letter was easier for you to write? Why?

2. In which letter did you use a more formal style?

Determining Subject, Purpose, and Audience

A Choose one of the following general subjects to write a paragraph about.

• your hometown

• your school

• your family

B Next, decide on a specific focus that interests you. Then determine your purpose and identify your audience.

Subject: _____

Focus: _____

Purpose: _____

Audience: _____

C Finally, write your paragraph.

_____

_____

_____

_____

_____

_____

_____

D Now find another focus of the same subject that you want to explore. Choose a different purpose for your writing and another audience.

Subject: _____

Focus: _____

Purpose: _____

Audience: _____

E Write a second paragraph.

_____

_____

_____

_____

_____

_____

_____

F How are your two paragraphs alike? How are they different?

THE WRITING PROCESS

Very few people pick up a pen or sit down at a computer and produce a perfect piece of writing on the first try. Most writers spend a lot of time thinking before they write and then work through a series of steps while they are composing. The final product is often the result of several careful revisions. It takes patience as well as skill to write well. You should think of writing as a process involving the following steps:

The Three-Step Writing Process

Step One: Prewriting
generating and organizing your ideas

↓

Step Two: Writing
using your ideas to write a first draft

↓

Step Three: Revising and Editing
improving what you have written

In this chapter, as well as the next two, you will learn more about these three steps.

STEP ONE: Prewriting

For many people, the hardest part of writing is *getting started*. Whether you enjoy writing or not, you will find it easier to write if you do some prewriting exercises to get started. Prewriting is a way to warm up your brain before you write, just as you warm up your car's engine before you drive.

Generating Ideas

Writers use a variety of prewriting techniques to generate ideas. Some of the most popular are *brainstorming, clustering, freewriting,* and *keeping a journal*.

© 1998 Randy Glasbergen. Email: randy@glasbergen.com

GLASBERGEN

**"Sometimes you get a brainstorm,
sometimes you just get the clouds."**

Brainstorming

Brainstorming is a quick way to generate a lot of ideas on a subject. The purpose is to come up with a list of as many ideas as possible without worrying about how you will use them. Your list may include words, phrases, sentences, or even questions. To brainstorm, follow these steps:

1. Begin with a broad topic.

2. Write down as many associations as you can in ten minutes.

3. Add more items by answering the questions: *Who? What? When? Where? Why?* and *How?*

4. Group the items on the list that go together.

5. Cross out items that do not belong.

Your list may seem unfocused as you are working on it. But you will later organize the items on your list and decide which ones you want to include in your essay and which you want to discard.

> **WRITER'S TIP:** Brainstorming
>
> Remember that when you brainstorm, the goal is to write down as many ideas as you can about the topic. Work as quickly as possible. Do not worry about choosing the ideas you like best. You will do that later.

Look at the list of ideas a student brainstormed about the topic of superstitions.

Topic: Superstitions	
my sister is very superstitious	wear lucky T-shirt for games
breaking a mirror	wedding superstitions
look for four-leaf clovers	eat eggs for breakfast on game day
superstitions in different countries	don't step on cracks
sit in center of room for tests	don't walk under ladders
finding a penny	animal superstitions
origin of superstitions	wear green when I fly
Friday the 13th	use lucky shoelaces in tennis shoes
always wear pearl necklace for tests	never start a trip on Friday
don't stay on 13th floor in a hotel	switch watch to right wrist for tests

After the student made her list, she read it over and decided to write an essay that focused on her personal superstitions. Then she crossed out items on the list that did not relate to the focus.

Topic: Superstitions

~~my sister is very superstitious~~	wear lucky T-shirt for games
breaking a mirror	~~wedding superstitions~~
look for four-leaf clovers	eat eggs for breakfast on game day
~~superstitions in different countries~~	don't step on cracks
sit in center of room for tests	don't walk under ladders
finding a penny	~~animal superstitions~~
~~origin of superstitions~~	wear green when I fly
Friday the 13th	use lucky shoelaces in tennis shoes
always wear pearl necklace for tests	never start a trip on Friday
don't stay on 13th floor in a hotel	switch watch to right wrist for tests

Next, she organized her personal superstitions into three categories: *tests*, *travel*, and *sports*.

Tests	Sports
always wear pearl necklace for tests	wear lucky T-shirt for games
sit in center of room for tests	use lucky shoelaces in tennis shoes
switch watch to right wrist for tests	eat eggs for breakfast on game day

Travel

never start a trip on Friday

don't stay on 13th floor in a hotel

wear green when I fly

Practicing Brainstorming

A In the following space, brainstorm a list of ideas for the general topic of *travel*.

B Now look at your list and choose a focus for a paragraph you could write. Cross out any items that do not relate to that focus. Finally, group similar ideas together.

Clustering

Clustering is a visual way of generating ideas. If you prefer to work with information visually, clustering might be a good technique for you. It shows the connections among your ideas using circles and lines. To cluster, follow these steps:

1. Write your topic in the center of a piece of paper and draw a circle around it.

2. Think about your topic and write any ideas that come to mind in circles around the main circle.

3. Connect these ideas to the center circle with lines.

4. Think about each of your new ideas, write more related ideas in circles around them, and connect them to their corresponding ideas with a line.

5. Repeat this process until you run out of ideas.

The following is an example of a cluster diagram one student made on the topic of *communication*. In this example, what topic or topics would he probably choose to write about? Why?

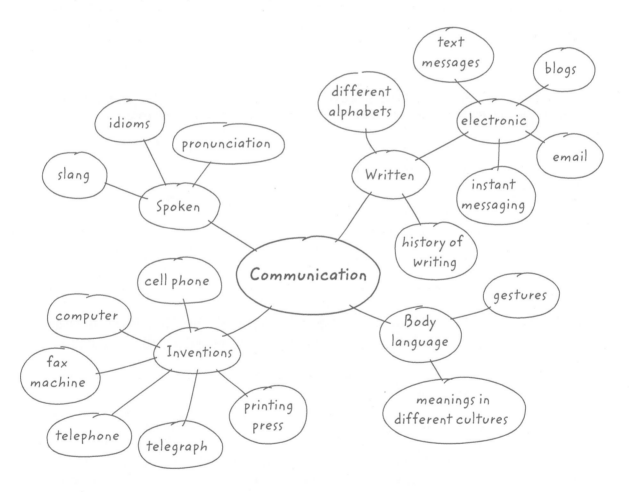

Practicing Clustering

PRACTICE **Use the following space to practice clustering for the topic of** *music.*

Freewriting

If you have a hard time finding a focus for a broad subject, freewriting might be a helpful technique for you. Freewriting is writing as much as you can, as fast as you can, without worrying about mistakes. To freewrite, follow these steps:

1. Write your general topic at the top of your page.

2. Start writing and write as much as you can, as fast as you can, for ten minutes.

3. Don't stop for any reason. Don't worry if your mind wanders away from your original idea. Don't worry about mistakes. Just keep writing. You can go back later and revise. Let your ideas flow.

4. If you can't think of anything, write, "My mind is blank, my mind is blank," or something similar, over and over again until a new thought comes into your mind.

5. Read your freewriting and see if there are any ideas you can develop into a paragraph.

A Read the freewriting sample on the topic of *fashion*.

> Fashion
>
> I love fashion. I buy lots of fashion magazines and love to look at what the models are wearing. I spend too much money on clothes, but I can't help it. I've always loved clothes and fashion. My favorite fashion designer is Marc Jacobs. I think fashion is like art. What you wear makes a personal statement. My favorite fashion magazine is "Vogue." I try to follow the latest trends in fashion. "What Not to Wear" and "Project Runway" are great fashion TV shows. I would love to be a fashion designer. I want to go to a fashion design school in New York City. My first choice is FIT (Fashion Institute of Technology). I hope I get accepted. What else can I say about fashion? I love trendy clothes. Sometimes I design and make my own clothes. My friends always ask me for fashion advice. Fashion is art. Fashion is creative. What else? Most of my friends are into fashion, too. We trade clothes and go shopping together. I want to be a famous fashion designer. I love to go to fashion shows. The clothes I wear reflect my personality.

B When you freewrite, your mind may jump around as new ideas come to you. You can see that as this author was writing, new and different ideas came into her mind. In this example, several different ideas could be developed into paragraphs. List some of them here.

_____

_____

_____

C Compare your list with a classmate's. Did you include the same items?

Practicing Freewriting

PRACTICE **A** Write for ten minutes on the subject of *your plans for the future.* Your teacher will tell you when to begin and when to stop writing.

_____

_____

_____

_____

_____

_____

_____

_____

_____

_____

_____

_____

_____

_____

_____

_____

_____

_____

_____

_____

_____

B Did you generate any ideas that you could now write a paragraph about? If so, what are they?

_____

_____

_____

_____

Keeping a Journal

You may find it helpful to keep a journal. When you are not given a specific subject to write on, you can refer to your journal for possible topics. To keep a journal, start by buying a notebook and writing in it for a few minutes every day. Write about anything you want. For example, you could write about the events of your day, the people you met, or your reaction to something that you heard, read, or saw.

Use your journal to record your daily thoughts and activities, and as a way of understanding yourself better. No matter what your reason for keeping a journal, you will find it a valuable source of ideas in your future writing and thinking.

Below is an example of a journal entry one student wrote.

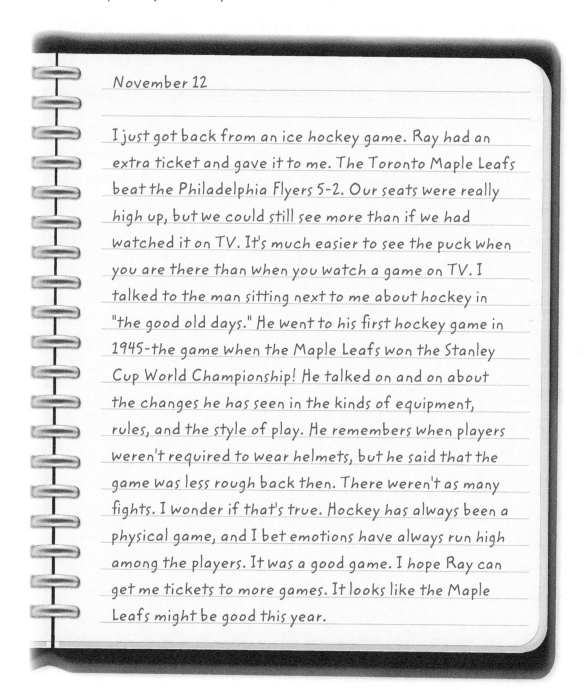

November 12

I just got back from an ice hockey game. Ray had an extra ticket and gave it to me. The Toronto Maple Leafs beat the Philadelphia Flyers 5-2. Our seats were really high up, but we could still see more than if we had watched it on TV. It's much easier to see the puck when you are there than when you watch a game on TV. I talked to the man sitting next to me about hockey in "the good old days." He went to his first hockey game in 1945-the game when the Maple Leafs won the Stanley Cup World Championship! He talked on and on about the changes he has seen in the kinds of equipment, rules, and the style of play. He remembers when players weren't required to wear helmets, but he said that the game was less rough back then. There weren't as many fights. I wonder if that's true. Hockey has always been a physical game, and I bet emotions have always run high among the players. It was a good game. I hope Ray can get me tickets to more games. It looks like the Maple Leafs might be good this year.

A List several of the general topics from this journal entry that the author might use to develop a paragraph.

_____

_____

_____

B Compare your list with a classmate's. Did you include the same items?

Practice Writing a Journal Entry

Use the following journal page to write your first journal entry. Write about something that happened to you recently.

Organizing

Part of prewriting is organizing your ideas. Making an informal outline of the ideas you generated from prewriting will help you organize your thoughts as you plan your paragraph. You can use your outline as a guide and refer to it while you are writing.

Here is an example of an outline based on the ideas generated from brainstorming on the topic of *superstitions*. Notice that the three headings in this outline are the same three categories determined in the brainstorming exercise on page 15.

Topic: My Superstitions

1. Superstitions about tests
   a. always wear pearl necklace for tests
   b. sit in center of room for tests
   c. switch watch to right wrist for tests

2. Superstitions about travel
   a. never start a trip on Friday
   b. don't stay on 13th floor in a hotel
   c. wear green when I fly

3. Superstitions about sports
   a. wear lucky T-shirt for games
   b. use lucky shoelaces in tennis shoes
   c. eat eggs for breakfast on game day

Preparing an Informal Outline

A **Prepare an informal outline based on the brainstorming exercise about *travel* on page 16. Write your focused topic on the line.**

Topic: _____

B Prepare an informal outline based on the topics in your clustering diagram on *music* on page 18. Write your focused topic on the line.

Topic: _____

CHAPTER HIGHLIGHTS

1. List and explain the three things you should consider when you write something.

   a. _____

   b. _____

   c. _____

2. What are the three basic steps in the writing process?

   a. _____

   b. _____

   c. _____

3. What are four common prewriting techniques you learned about in this chapter?

   a. _____

   b. _____

   c. _____

   d. _____

4. What is one way you can organize the ideas you generated from prewriting?

   _____

Paragraph Writing: Write paragraphs using time order, spatial order, and order of importance

After you have spent some time thinking about your topic and doing the necessary prewriting, you are ready for the next step in the writing process: writing your paragraph.

© Randy Glasbergen / glasbergen.com
GLASBERGEN

PARAGRAPH BASICS

Most writing that is longer than a few sentences is organized into paragraphs. A

paragraph is a group of sentences that all relate to a single topic. Since paragraphs can

include many different kinds of information, there are many different types of paragraphs.

For example, some paragraphs describe people, places, or ideas. Other paragraphs

explain how to do or make something, narrate a series of events, compare or contrast

two things, or describe causes and effects. Some paragraphs are part of longer pieces

of writing, such as an essay, an article, a chapter of a book. Other paragraphs are stand-

alone paragraphs. In this chapter, you will practice writing stand-alone paragraphs.

The Parts of a Paragraph

Remember that a paragraph is a group of sentences about one topic. Most stand-alone paragraphs have three main parts: **the topic sentence, the supporting sentences, and the concluding sentence**. Most stand-alone paragraphs also have a title.

The topic of the paragraph is usually stated in the first sentence. This sentence is called the *topic sentence*. The other sentences add details to the topic. They are called *supporting sentences*. Some paragraphs also have a *concluding sentence*, which summarizes the ideas of the paragraph. It is the last sentence of the paragraph.

Read the following paragraph about superstitions. It is based on the outline on page 23.

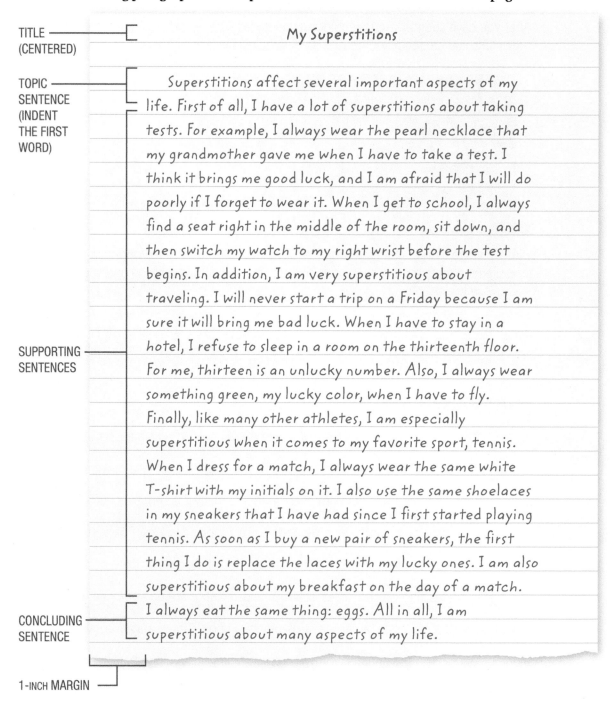

TITLE (CENTERED)

TOPIC SENTENCE (INDENT THE FIRST WORD)

SUPPORTING SENTENCES

CONCLUDING SENTENCE

1-INCH MARGIN

My Superstitions

Superstitions affect several important aspects of my life. First of all, I have a lot of superstitions about taking tests. For example, I always wear the pearl necklace that my grandmother gave me when I have to take a test. I think it brings me good luck, and I am afraid that I will do poorly if I forget to wear it. When I get to school, I always find a seat right in the middle of the room, sit down, and then switch my watch to my right wrist before the test begins. In addition, I am very superstitious about traveling. I will never start a trip on a Friday because I am sure it will bring me bad luck. When I have to stay in a hotel, I refuse to sleep in a room on the thirteenth floor. For me, thirteen is an unlucky number. Also, I always wear something green, my lucky color, when I have to fly. Finally, like many other athletes, I am especially superstitious when it comes to my favorite sport, tennis. When I dress for a match, I always wear the same white T-shirt with my initials on it. I also use the same shoelaces in my sneakers that I have had since I first started playing tennis. As soon as I buy a new pair of sneakers, the first thing I do is replace the laces with my lucky ones. I am also superstitious about my breakfast on the day of a match. I always eat the same thing: eggs. All in all, I am superstitious about many aspects of my life.

STEP TWO OF THE WRITING PROCESS: Writing

As you write the first draft of your paragraph, you can use the ideas you generated from prewriting and your outline as a guide. Remember that writing the first draft is only one step in the writing process. The first draft is not the finished product. The goal of the first draft is to put your ideas in writing.

As you write the first draft of your paragraph, remember that you need to do several things:

1. State your point clearly in a topic sentence.

2. Support your point with adequate information.

3. Develop unity by making sure all your sentences relate to the topic.

4. Create coherence by organizing your sentences logically, including transitions, and repeating key words.

TOPIC SENTENCES

When you write a paragraph in English, the first thing you need to do is to state your main point in one clear sentence called *the topic sentence*. The rest of the paragraph should develop and support the point you made in the topic sentence.

The topic sentence is usually the first sentence of a paragraph. It is the most important one in your paragraph because it controls all of the other sentences. A topic sentence must do two things: state the *topic* (main idea) and identify the *focus* (main emphasis) of the paragraph.

A good topic sentence < states the **topic** of the paragraph.
                         identifies the **focus**.

Look at these two topic sentences.

Nuclear power is our greatest hope for solving the energy crisis.

1. What is the topic of this sentence? _____

2. What is the focus? _____

Nuclear power is a huge threat to life on the planet.

1. What is the topic of this sentence? _____

2. What is the focus? _____

Notice that both sentences have the same topic, but the focus is different.

Analyzing Topic Sentences

PRACTICE **Read the topic sentences below. Underline the topic and draw a circle around the focus.**

1. Mahatma Gandhi was an influential leader.

2. Email is a great way to stay in touch with your family and friends.

3. The clothes we wear often reflect a lot about our personality.

4. The Japanese subway system is very efficient.

5. Television commercials are often insulting to women.

6. My older brother is a perfectionist.

7. The laws on child abuse should be strictly enforced.

8. Being a twin has both advantages and disadvantages.

9. The new shopping mall has brought many economic benefits to our community.

10. Golf is a difficult sport to master.

A good topic sentence should not be too general or too specific. If your topic sentence is too general, you will not be able to support the topic in one paragraph. If it is too specific, you won't have enough to write about in the rest of the paragraph.

Look at the following topic sentence.

Exercising is fun.

This statement is too general to develop adequately into one paragraph. There is too much to say about the topic.

Now look at this topic sentence.

I swim laps for thirty minutes every morning.

This statement is too specific to be developed into a paragraph. There isn't enough to say about the topic.

Finally, look at this topic sentence. It would be easy to support this sentence in one paragraph. It is not too general or too specific.

Exercising every morning has several positive effects on my health.

Evaluating Topic Sentences

PRACTICE **Work with a partner. Read the following sentences. Write *OK* by those that are effective topic sentences. Write *S* by the sentences that are not good topic sentences because they are too specific. Write *G* by the sentences that are not good topic sentences because they are too general.**

_____ 1. My round-trip plane ticket to Ankara, Turkey, cost more than $950.

_____ 2. Many people have hobbies.

_____ **3.** American music reflects the native music of many of its immigrant groups.

_____ **4.** Music is important to society.

_____ **5.** Genetically altered food is unacceptable for several reasons.

_____ **6.** Mark Zuckerberg founded Facebook®.

_____ **7.** Vacations are expensive.

_____ **8.** Learning to read and write in Chinese is difficult for students from other countries.

_____ **9.** Talking on cell phones in public places is rude.

_____ **10.** The Chinese language has more than 50,000 characters.

_____ **11.** Zebras have stripes.

_____ **12.** Cutting your children's hair is easy and can save you a lot of money.

_____ **13.** Learning to write in a foreign language can be frustrating.

_____ **14.** There are many programs on television.

_____ **15.** My new car is a Toyota Prius.

Writing Topic Sentences

PRACTICE **Write a topic sentence for each of the following paragraphs. Be sure that each one states the main point and the focus. Then, in small groups, compare and discuss your topic sentences.**

1.
Reactions to Jet Lag

Your reaction to jet lag depends on several factors. Symptoms may last for one day or several days and vary greatly in severity. One factor is the number of time zones you crossed. Your jet lag will probably be worse if you crossed several time zones. Another factor is whether you flew east to west or west to east. It is easier to adjust after an east-to-west flight. Personality factors also affect how easily you adapt to the new time. For example, "night" people adapt more easily than "morning" people. Extroverts adjust more easily than introverts. Flexible people who don't mind changes have fewer problems than inflexible people who are rigid and don't like change. Younger people suffer less than older people. Finally, healthier people usually get over jet lag more easily than people who are sick. As you can see, several factors determine your reaction to jet lag.

2.
Information in English Dictionaries

_____ For one thing, an English dictionary tells you how to spell and pronounce each word correctly. It also tells you the meaning of each word. Since many words in English have more than one meaning, a dictionary gives all of the meanings. In addition, a dictionary identifies the part of speech (noun, verb, adjective, adverb, and so on) of each word. Some English dictionaries also include information about the etymology (origin and history) of the words. Finally, many dictionaries give synonyms and antonyms of the word you are looking up.

3.
The Effects of Climate on Our Lives

_____ For instance, climate affects the kinds of clothes we wear and even the colors we choose to wear. Since climate affects the kinds of crops we can grow, it influences our eating habits. Architecture is also affected by climate. Engineers and architects must think about climate when they make decisions about the construction, materials, and design of buildings. Even our choices in transportation are determined by the climate in which we live. Climate plays a big part in economic development, too. A climate that is too hot, too cold, or too dry makes farming, industry, and transportation difficult and slows down economic development. All in all, climate affects many aspects of our lives.

4.
Gift-giving Customs

_____ Whether you are a tourist, a student, or a businessperson, it is important to know the gift-giving customs of the country you are visiting. For example, if you are invited for dinner, flowers are a safe and appreciated gift throughout the world. In much of Europe, however, red roses symbolize romance and would be inappropriate. In Austria and Germany, it is considered bad luck to receive an even number of flowers. If you are giving a gift in Hong Kong, you should avoid clocks, which symbolize death, and scissors or knives, which indicate the end of the relationship. In Japan, you can impress your hosts by paying attention to the Japanese rules for gift-giving: Always wrap the gift, but not in white paper, as white symbolizes death. In addition, never give four of anything, since the Japanese word for the number four is also the word for death. As in Korea and much of Asia, do not expect your gift to be opened until after you have left. In conclusion, no matter where in the world you are, you will feel more comfortable if you take the time to learn some of the local gift-giving customs.

5.
A Prestigious Prize

_____ Since 1901, the Nobel Prize has been awarded annually to scientists, authors, scholars, and peacemakers for outstanding accomplishments in science, literature, peace, and economics. The prizes were first established in the will of Swedish scientist Alfred Nobel, who invented dynamite in 1895. Originally, the Nobel Prize was awarded for excellence in five categories: physics, chemistry, literature, physiology or medicine, and peace. Today, the awards have expanded to fields such as economics and public health. Each Nobel winner receives a medal, a personal diploma, and a cash award. The award ceremony has become a true international event as recipients come from all over the world. All in all, it is no wonder that many people consider the Nobel Prize to be the most prestigious award given for intellectual achievement in the world.

WRITER'S TIP: Topic Sentences

While you are writing a paragraph, you should look back at your topic sentence. This will help you to avoid including any information that is not related to the topic sentence.

SUPPORTING SENTENCES

Support Your Point

After you have stated your main point in the topic sentence, you need to support it in the sentences that follow. These sentences are called supporting sentences. The supporting sentences can include reasons, facts, and examples. Try to make your supporting sentences as specific as possible. Supporting sentences that are vague or that just repeat the point you made in the topic sentence are not effective.

> **WRITER'S TIP:** Using Facts, Reasons, and Examples
>
> As a writer, it is your job to provide enough support to prove the point you made in your topic sentence. Remember to support your point with:
> - facts;
> - reasons; and
> - examples.

Analyzing Paragraphs for Support

A **Read the following two paragraphs. Both begin with the same topic sentence, but only one develops it with enough specific support.**

Paragraph 1

> ## Our Trip to Costa Rica
>
> Our family trip to Costa Rica last summer was very exciting. Every day we saw something new and different. One day we went hiking. Another day we took a rafting trip down a river. We saw lots of unusual plants and animals that we had never seen before. We did many things that we will never forget. Everyone agreed that this was the best trip we have ever taken.

Paragraph 2

> ## Our Trip to Costa Rica
>
> Our family trip to Costa Rica last summer was very exciting. We were there for two weeks, and not a day went by without something unusual happening. On our second day, a boa constrictor swam right in front of us while we were rafting down the Río Claro. Another day, spider monkeys threw branches at us deep in the rain forest. Hiking on the primitive trails in Corcovado National Park, we saw brilliant scarlet macaws and toucans with huge yellow beaks. Indeed, whenever we look at the pictures from our trip, we all agree that it was the most exciting one we have ever taken.

B **Which paragraph do you think provides enough specific support?** _____

C **Underline examples of specific support in the paragraph you chose.**

Evaluating Support

Read the following sets of paragraphs and answer the questions. Only one paragraph in each set develops the main point with adequate support.

Set 1

Paragraph 1

Expensive Car Repairs

The repairs on my car were much more expensive than I had anticipated. When I saw the final bill, I was in shock. It was twice as much as I had planned on. I had to pay $395 to get the brakes repaired and another $100 to get the wheels aligned. The engine oil change was $30, and the replacement of the air filter was another $20. As a result, the next time my car needs repairs, I'll go to a different mechanic.

Paragraph 2

Expensive Car Repairs

The repairs on my car were much more expensive than I had anticipated. The mechanic did a good job, but I think I was overcharged for everything. I never imagined that the final bill would be so high. In fact, I had to borrow money from my friend to pay it. As a result, the next time my car needs repairs, I'll go to a different mechanic.

1. Which paragraph provides more specific support?

   _____

2. What four supporting details does the author include in that paragraph?

   _____   _____

   _____   _____

Set 2

Paragraph 1

A Difficult Course

My chemistry course is very difficult and time-consuming. The professor doesn't seem to realize that chemistry isn't the only course we're taking. He gives lots of homework and too much reading. The worst thing is that his lectures are really boring. I'm not interested in chemistry, so I hate reading the textbook. I know I'm not the only student complaining about this course. In conclusion, I wish I had never registered for this course.

Paragraph 2

A Difficult Course

My chemistry course is very difficult and time-consuming. First of all, we're responsible for two labs every week, which means a minimum of ten hours a week in the lab. To make matters worse, the professor gives at least three tests per month. The questions are very tricky, and we have to memorize long, complicated formulas. Finally, the reading load of the course is also quite heavy—as much as twenty-five pages a night. I often spend all my free time doing the required reading. In conclusion, my difficult chemistry course takes up too much of my time.

1. Which paragraph provides more specific support?

   _____

2. What four supporting details does the author include in that paragraph?

   _____

   _____

   _____

   _____

Paragraph 1

The Effects of Climate Change

It is clear that the effects of climate change on the environment could be disastrous. For one thing, deserts will become hotter and drier and continue to expand. Rising seas, caused in part by the melting of half the world's mountain glaciers, will flood low-lying islands and coasts, threatening millions of people. Global warming will change the climate regionally and globally, altering natural vegetation and affecting crop production. Indeed, all kinds of plants and forests, from the tropics to the Arctic tundra, will undergo extreme transformation. Finally, higher temperatures could also cause more extreme storms, allowing tropical diseases to invade temperate areas. As you can see, the effects of climate change are alarming.

Paragraph 2

The Effects of Climate Change

There is little question that a climate change such as warming of the atmosphere would have profound environmental effects. Something needs to be done about this. Once it begins, the trend toward warmer temperatures could be disastrous. It would speed up the melting of ice caps and raise sea levels. An increase in atmospheric carbon dioxide of 10 percent over the past century has led some authorities to predict a long-term warming of the Earth's climate. This warming could have a severe impact on our environment and the world as we know it. In 2015, more than 10,000 scientists, environmental activists, and government officials from 187 countries met in Paris, France, for the United Nations Climate Change Conference. Most scientists now agree that climate change could have serious environmental consequences. It is time to take the problem seriously.

1. Which paragraph is vague, repetitive, and lacks enough support to prove the point?

_____

2. Which sentences in that paragraph simply restate the topic?

_____

_____

_____

3. Which sentences are true but do not really support the point that global warming could have a profound effect on the environment?

_____

_____

_____

Writing Supporting Sentences

PRACTICE **A** **Write three supporting sentences for each of the following topic sentences.**

1. I am terrible at doing the laundry.

   a. *I forget to separate the colored clothes from the white ones and end up with gray socks.*

   b. *I rarely read the cleaning instructions and have ruined clothes by putting them in the washing machine instead of dry-cleaning them.*

   c. *I often shrink my favorite shirts because I leave them in the dryer for too long.*

2. I love trying food from different countries.

   a. _____

   b. _____

   c. _____

3. Summer (or spring, fall, winter) is my favorite season.

   a. _____

   b. _____

   c. _____

4. There is too much violence on television.

   a. _____

   b. _____

   c. _____

5. There are several ways to conserve energy.

   a. _____

   b. _____

   c. _____

6. It is almost impossible to study in my dormitory (or at home).

   a. _____

   b. _____

   c. _____

B **Choose the topic sentence that you have the best support for and develop it into a paragraph.**

_____

_____

_____

_____

_____

_____

_____

_____

_____

_____

_____

C **Exchange paragraphs with a partner. Does your partner's topic sentence have enough support? If not, give suggestions for adding support.**

Supplying Specific Details

To write a fully developed paragraph, often you will need to provide specific details to strengthen your main supporting points. Each of the following paragraphs has a topic sentence and three or four main supporting points. With a classmate, complete the paragraphs by adding your own specific details to clarify each supporting point.

1. My mother nags me constantly. For one thing, my room is never clean enough to suit her. _Although I hang up my clothes once a week, she expects me to put them away every night before I go to bed. She also hates it if I leave any food, wrappers, or soda cans in my room._ In addition, she never thinks I've spent enough time on my schoolwork.

    _____

    _____

    Finally, she is always telling me to improve my appearance. _____

_____

_____

As you can see, my mother is always nagging me.

2.　　After my grandfather moved in with us, I began to realize the benefits of living with an older

person. First of all, he has told me a lot of stories about our family history. _____

_____

_____

_____ In addition, since my grandfather is retired, he has been able to

spend a lot of time helping me with my schoolwork. _____

_____

_____

_____ Most importantly, I've learned to appreciate the special qualities

an older person can have. _____

_____

_____

3.　　There are many ways to economize on a trip to _____ and still have a

good time. First, you can shop around for the best airfare. _____

_____

_____

_____ Once you get there, you do not need to stay in the most

expensive hotels. _____

_____

_____

You can also economize on food. _____

_____

_____

Finally, you should take advantage of all the free cultural and historical offerings. _____

_____

_____

_____

CONCLUDING SENTENCES

Some paragraphs end with a concluding sentence. This sentence often restates the main idea of the paragraph using different words. It summarizes the main points of the paragraph or makes a final comment on the topic. The concluding sentence helps readers because it reminds them of the main point and because it signals the end of the paragraph.

Here are some common ways to begin a concluding sentence. Notice that these words or phrases are followed by a comma.

All in all,

As you can see,

In conclusion,

In short,

Indeed,

As a result,

Concluding sentences are common in stand-alone paragraphs, but they are not necessary for every type of paragraph. For example, some very short paragraphs do not need a concluding sentence. Also, paragraphs that are part of longer pieces of writing often do not have concluding sentences.

A **Read the paragraph. Underline the concluding sentence.**

The Advantages of Credit Cards

Credit cards have a lot of advantages. First of all, credit cards are convenient because you don't have to carry a lot of cash around. You can buy the products and services you need even if you do not have cash in your pocket. In addition, credit cards are very helpful in emergencies. Finally, you can become a better money manager as you learn to use credit cards responsibly. As you can see, there are many advantages of using credit cards.

B **What words did the author use from the topic sentence?**

C **Work with a partner. Write a concluding sentence for each of the paragraphs on pages 36–38. Then compare your concluding sentences with those of another pair.**

WRITER'S TIP: Concluding Sentences

When you write a concluding sentence, you can repeat words or use synonyms of words from the topic sentence.

TITLES

Many stand-alone paragraphs have a title. The purpose of the title is to give the reader an idea what the paragraph is about. A title of a paragraph tells the main idea in a few words. If a paragraph is part of a longer piece of writing, it does not need a title.

Most titles are a short phrase or even just one word. Here are some things to remember when you write titles:

- Titles are not complete sentences.
- Always capitalize the first and last words of a title.
- Capitalize all other important words in the title including nouns, verbs, and adjectives. Do not capitalize articles (*a*, *an*, *the*) or prepositions (for example, *to*, *from*, *at*, *with*)
- Do not use a period at the end of a title. Do not use quotation marks (" ") around the title. But you may use a question mark (?) or an exclamation point (!).
- Center the title over the paragraph.

PRACTICE **A** **Correct the titles.**

1. Benefits OF Solar Energy

   _____

2. MY NEW ROOMMATE

   _____

3. "How to change a tire"

   _____

4. I enjoy Spending Time With My Friends.

   _____

5. It is Important to Dress Appropriately for a Job Interview.

   _____

B **Work with a partner. Write titles for the paragraphs on pages 36–38. Then share your titles with the rest of the class. Your teacher will write the titles on the blackboard.**

WRITER'S TIP: Paragraph Titles

It is often easier to write the title for your paragraph after you have written the first draft. Remember to keep your audience in mind as you write your title.

DEVELOP UNITY

In addition to writing a clear topic sentence and providing adequate support, you need to make sure your paragraph has unity. When every sentence relates to the main idea by explaining it or proving it, the paragraph has unity. If a sentence does not relate to the main idea, it is irrelevant. You should eliminate irrelevant sentences from your paragraph.

Read the next two paragraphs. Notice that the first one has unity because all the sentences relate to the topic sentence, but the second one includes some information that does not relate to the main idea.

Paragraph 1

A Terrible Location

My apartment is in a terrible location. First of all, it is too far away from the important stores and services. It is several miles from a grocery store, bank, post office, library, or pharmacy. To make matters worse, there is no convenient public transportation in my neighborhood. The one bus line near my apartment runs only one bus an hour and has a very limited route. Almost everywhere I need to go involves changing buses and takes a lot of time. In addition, my apartment is in a high-crime area. Gangs of teenagers roam the streets, threatening the neighbors. Last month alone, eight robberies took place on our block. The elderly woman who lives next door had her purse snatched while she was walking her dog. Finally, because my apartment is near an industrial area, the pollution is awful. A nearby chemical plant causes so much smog that it is often hard for me to breathe. I agree with people who say that when you are looking for an apartment, location is everything.

All the sentences in the first paragraph support and develop the single point stated in the topic sentence: "My apartment is in a terrible location." The paragraph has unity.

Paragraph 2

A Great Location

I love the location of my new house. For one thing, it's in a very safe neighborhood, and I'm not afraid to go out alone. There's almost no crime, and most people don't even lock their doors. In addition, the neighborhood is in a convenient location. Lots of stores, schools, and restaurants are nearby. Within a few miles, there is also a library, health and fitness center, and movie theater. Most of all, I really like the people who live in this neighborhood. They're friendly and helpful and seem to want to keep our community safe and clean. My new house is roomy, comfortable, and sunny, but I need to buy some more furniture. I definitely chose a great location to buy a house.

The focus of this paragraph is expressed in the first sentence: "I love the location of my new house." Most of the other sentences develop and support this sentence. But the next to last sentence, "My new house is roomy, comfortable, and sunny, but I need to buy some more furniture." has nothing to do with location. It is not related to the topic. It should *not* be included in this paragraph because it is irrelevant.

Identifying Irrelevant Sentences

PRACTICE Ⓐ Read the paragraph a student wrote about Boston's annual New Year's Eve celebration. Decide which sentences do not belong in the paragraph because they do not support the topic sentence. Cross out the irrelevant sentences.

First Night

Every year on New Year's Eve, Boston hosts a community celebration called First Night so people can celebrate the New Year together. Boston was the first city in the United States to launch a special event to celebrate New Year's Eve. First Night attracts more than 1.5 million people. For the twenty dollar cost of a First Night button, people gain general admission to many different events. Boston is the higher-education capital of the United States. The two largest universities within the city itself are Boston University and Northeastern University, and in nearby Cambridge are Harvard University and the Massachusetts Institute of Technology. The evening begins with a grand costumed parade around the Boston Common and ends at midnight with fireworks over Boston Harbor. In between, there are more than 250 performances of international music, dance, and theater, as well as puppetry and many films to choose from. Boston is also host to the well-known Boston Marathon, which is run in April. Two hundred cities and towns in the United States, Canada, and Australia have now launched celebrations like the one in Boston for New Year's Eve.

Ⓑ Which sentences did you cross out? Compare the ones you deleted with those your classmates deleted.

C Now read this paragraph and underline the topic sentence. Then decide which sentences are irrelevant and cross them out.

Are You a Nervous Flier?

If you are a nervous flier, you can do several things to reduce the stress. First of all, educate yourself about flying. You might consider taking a Fearful Flier workshop. The purpose of this workshop is to help you become more comfortable with flying by replacing the myths about flying with facts, such as what makes a plane fly and how crews are trained. The workshop will also teach you how to deal with your fears. There are also many interesting workshops you can take to relieve stress at work. Planning ahead for your flight is a second way to cut down on stress. Leave plenty of time to get to the airport. Remember there may be long lines, so be sure to get to the airport early. If possible, check in and print out your boarding pass at home to save time and avoid hassles. Learn the security procedures so you will know what you can and can't take through security. Many airports have shops and restaurants where you can spend time between flights. Third, communicate your fears. Tell the check-in person that you are a nervous flier, and you may be able to board early. Also talk to the flight crew. If crew members know that you are anxious, they will make more of an effort to put you at ease. Another tip to relieve anxiety is to stay loose, both physically and mentally. Wear loose, comfortable clothing and try to relax. Flex your hands and feet. Get up and walk around. Unfortunately, the food served on many flights is unappetizing. Keep your mind active, too. Bring along a good book, some magazines, or a lot of absorbing work so you won't dwell on your fears.

D Which sentences did you cross out? Compare the ones you deleted with the ones your classmates deleted.

CREATE COHERENCE

As a writer, you need to be sure your ideas flow smoothly and logically from one sentence to the next. When you do this, your paragraph will have coherence. Readers can follow the main ideas more easily when your paragraph has coherence.

To create coherence, you should do several things:

- Organize the sentences so that the order of ideas makes sense.
- Use transitions to help the reader understand how the ideas in your paragraph are connected.
- Repeat key (important) words and phrases.

Organize Your Ideas

The way you arrange your information depends on the kind of paragraph you are writing. For example, if you are telling a story, the logical organization of sentences will be chronological—that is, arranged according to *time order*. If you are describing what your bedroom looks like, you will organize the details according to where things are located. In this case, you will use *spatial order*. Finally, if you are discussing examples, causes, effects, or reasons, you will probably use *order of importance*. With this type of organization, you might begin with the least important item and end with the most important one.

COMMON METHODS OF ORGANIZATION	
TIME ORDER	Use this method when you tell a story, describe what happened, give instructions, or explain a process. Organize the events in the story or process as they occur in time.
SPATIAL ORDER	Use this method when you describe a place or what something looks like. Choose a starting point and describe where things are located in relation to your starting point, such as left or right, above or below, or in front of or behind.
ORDER OF IMPORTANCE	Use this method to organize ideas, examples, and reasons for emphasis. You can order them in various ways, for example, from least to most important, from general to specific, from most to least familiar, or from simplest to most complex.

Identify the method of organization used in each paragraph.

1.
A Good Classroom Layout

My anthropology teacher, Mr. Carter, likes a classroom layout that invites interaction among students. He sets up the physical space so that it encourages us to interact with each other as much as possible. Mr. Carter's desk is in the center of the room with the students' desks in a U-shape. That means that the students surround him and everyone can always see everyone else. As you walk into the room, you will notice a large window on the back wall with bookshelves on both sides. If you look to the left, you will see the bulletin boards, which take up almost the entire wall. To the right is the computer station with enough computers for ten students. Behind you as you face the window are the chalkboards. Above the boards, ready to be rolled down whenever we need them, are many different maps of the world. This type of classroom may not work for every teacher, but it works very well for Mr. Carter.

Method of organization: _____

2.
Homing Pigeons

Homing pigeons have been known to fly more than 994 miles (1,600 kilometers) in two days. How do they do it? Homing pigeons use a combination of navigational cues to find their way to distant places. One cue they use is the position of the sun. Using the sun as their compass, they compensate for its apparent movement, see both ultraviolet and polarized light, and employ a backup compass for cloudy days. Another navigational cue homing pigeons use is based on their mental map of the landmarks in their home areas. Even if a pigeon is taken hundreds of kilometers from its loft in total darkness, it will depart almost directly for home when it is released. The most important cue homing pigeons use is the magnetic field of Earth. Their magnetic compass enables homing pigeons to navigate on cloudy and foggy days.

Method of organization: _____

3.
The Earth's Oceans

      The story of the Earth's oceans began 200 million years ago when the Earth was just a ball of hot rock. At first, its surface was covered with erupting volcanoes, which released huge amounts of gas, including a gas made up of water particles, called water vapor. Eventually the Earth cooled, causing the water vapor to turn back into liquid water and fall from the skies as torrential rain. The rain lasted for thousands and thousands of years. Finally, rainwater filled all the hollows around the Earth's surface, forming oceans and seas. Today, water covers almost three-quarters of Earth's surface, and more than 97 percent of all this water is stored in the Earth's four huge oceans: the Pacific, Atlantic, Indian, and Arctic Oceans.

      Method of organization: _____

Use Transitions

Expressions such as *next*, *for example*, and *in back of* are called *transitions*. Transitions are signals that show the connection between one idea and the next. They are important because they guide the reader through a paragraph and make it easier to understand. In this chapter, you will learn some transitions for indicating time relationships, explaining spatial relationships, listing additional ideas, and giving examples. In later chapters, you will learn other kinds of transitions.

TRANSITION SIGNALS THAT INDICATE TIME RELATIONSHIPS

after	eventually	next
as	ever since	recently
as soon as	every year	since
at last	finally	soon afterward
at this point	first	the next day (week, month, year)
before	from then on	then
by the time	in between	today
during	later	while
earlier	meanwhile	

TRANSITION SIGNALS THAT INDICATE SPATIAL RELATIONSHIPS

above	beside	near
across	between	next to
at the center	in back of	to the left
behind	in front of	to the right
below		

TRANSITION SIGNALS THAT INDICATE ADDITIONAL IDEAS

also	furthermore	next
another reason	in addition	one reason
besides	last	second
finally	last but not least	the most important reason
first	moreover	the third reason
first of all	most importantly	

TRANSITION SIGNALS THAT INDICATE EXAMPLES

as an illustration	for instance	such as
especially	specifically	to illustrate
for example		

PRACTICE **A** **Underline transitions in this paragraph.**

An International Language

English is only one of the world's 6,800 languages, but it is rapidly becoming a truly international language. First of all, English is the native language of more than 400 million people scattered across every continent. In fact, English is used in some way by one out of seven human beings around the globe, making it the most widely spoken language in history. Approximately 50 percent of the world's books are published in English. In addition, three-quarters of all mail, faxes, and electronic messages are written in English. English is also the main language of science, technology, and international business. More than half of all scientific and technical journals are written in English, and more than 80 percent of the information stored in computers around the world is in English. More than half of all business deals in Europe are conducted in English, and many more are negotiated in English in other parts of the international business community. Finally, English is the language of sports and entertainment. For example, it is the official language of both the Olympics and the Miss Universe Pageant. English is the language of more than 60 percent of the world's radio and TV programs. More than ever before, English is now the most widely used and studied language of the world.

B Look back at the three paragraphs on pages 43 and 44. Underline the transitions and answer the following questions.

1. Which kind of transition signals did the author use in the paragraph describing the classroom?

   _____

2. Which kind of transition signals did the author use to discuss the navigational cues of homing pigeons?

   _____

3. Which kind of transition signals did the author use to explain the formation of oceans?

   _____

Repeat Key Words or Phrases

When you write a paragraph, you should repeat key words. This will help you stay on track, and it will also help the reader stay focused on your topic. The key word is usually mentioned in the topic sentence.

WRITER'S TIP: Synonyms

If repeating the same word over and over makes your paragraph boring, you can use synonyms for the key words. You can also use pronouns to replace some key nouns.

Reread the paragraph *My Superstitions*. Underline the key word in the topic sentence. How many times does the author repeat this word? _____

My Superstitions

Superstitions affect several important aspects of my life. First of all, I have a lot of superstitions about taking tests. For example, I always wear the pearl necklace that my grandmother gave me when I have to take a test. I think it brings me good luck, and I am afraid that I will do poorly if I forget to wear it. When I get to school, I always find a seat right in the middle of the room, sit down, and then switch my watch to my right wrist before the test begins. In addition, I am very superstitious about traveling. I will never start a trip on a Friday because I am sure it will bring me bad luck. When I have to stay in a hotel, I refuse to sleep in a room on the thirteenth floor. For me, thirteen is an unlucky number. Also, I always wear something green, my lucky color, when I have to fly. Finally, like many other athletes, I am especially superstitious when it comes to my favorite sport, tennis. When I dress for a match, I always wear the same white T-shirt with my initials on it. I also use the same shoelaces in my sneakers that I have had since I first started playing tennis. As soon as I buy a new pair of sneakers, the first thing I do is replace the laces with my lucky ones. I am also superstitious about my breakfast on the day of a match. I always eat the same thing: eggs. All in all, I am superstitious about many aspects of my life.

Practicing Coherence

PRACTICE **A** **Think about the steps involved in planning a weekend trip to another city. Make a list of the steps and arrange them in time order.**

Steps:

* _____

* _____

* _____

* _____

* _____

B **Write a paragraph based on your list. Begin with a topic sentence and use transitions to connect your ideas. Repeat important words or phrases. Include a title.**

_____

_____

_____

_____

_____

_____

_____

_____

_____

_____

C What could someone learn about you from looking at your bedroom? Make a list of the items you want to describe and their placement in the room. Arrange your list according to spatial order.

Items:

- _____
- _____
- _____
- _____
- _____

D Using spatial order, write a paragraph describing how your bedroom reflects your personality. Begin with a topic sentence and use transitions to connect your ideas. Repeat key words. Include a title.

_____

_____

_____

_____

_____

_____

_____

_____

_____

_____

E If you could live in any time period (past, present, or future), which one would you pick? Choose one and make a list of your reasons. Arrange the list in order of importance. You can begin or end with your most important reason.

Reasons:

- _____
- _____
- _____
- _____
- _____

F Write a paragraph based on your list. Begin with a topic sentence and use transitions to connect your ideas. Remember to repeat key words. Include a title.

_____

_____

_____

_____

_____

_____

_____

_____

_____

_____

ON YOUR OWN

A Choose one of the following topics to develop into a paragraph.

- qualities of a good doctor
- description of your flag
- reasons you like (or do not like) modern art
- reasons cigarette advertising should (or should not) be banned
- ways to get good grades
- how to prepare your favorite salad, soup, or dessert
- the perfect design of a baseball field, basketball court, tennis court, or soccer field
- the benefits of having a job that requires a lot of travel
- how to make new friends
- the disadvantages of working for a large company
- description of your ideal kitchen

B Use one of the prewriting techniques you practiced in Chapter 1 to get you started: brainstorming, clustering, freewriting, or writing in a journal.

C Organize the ideas you generated by preparing a simple outline.

D Write a topic sentence for your paragraph that has a single focus.

E On a separate piece of paper, write the first draft. Remember to develop each of your supporting points with specific details. Use transitions to help guide your reader from one idea to the next. Repeat key words.

CHAPTER HIGHLIGHTS

Complete the paragraph below by filling in the blanks. You do not have to use exact words from the chapter as long as the ideas are correct.

There are several things to remember about writing a good paragraph in English. A paragraph is a group of sentences about _____ 1. . The most important sentence in a paragraph is the _____ 2. . This sentence _____ 3. everything else that goes into your paragraph. All the other sentences _____ 4. by _____ 5. . The topic sentence should state the _____ 6. and _____ 7. . You will always need to support your topic sentences with _____ 8. . In addition to a clear topic sentence and adequate support, a good paragraph must also have a _____ 9. and _____ 10. . A paragraph has unity if all the supporting details _____ 11. to the topic. A paragraph also needs to be easy to understand. This means it should have a logical organization. Three basic ways to organize information in a paragraph are by _____ 12. , _____ 13. , and _____ 14. . A good paragraph also needs _____ 15. to connect ideas.

LEARNING OUTCOME

Essay Writing: Use the writing process to write an essay about the pressures of being a student

Once you have put your ideas on paper, you should feel proud of your accomplishment. But your work is not done yet. You still need to see how effectively you have communicated your thoughts. It is time to turn to the important step of revising and editing.

WillWriteForChocolate.com   ©2007 Debbie Ridpath Ohi - Twitter: @inkyelbows

STEP THREE OF THE WRITING PROCESS:
Revising and Editing

REVISING

Don't forget that writing is a process. An important part of that process is *revising*. The word *revision* is a combination of the word *vision* and the prefix *re-*, which means "again." When you revise, you "see again," that is, you look at your writing again to see how you can improve it.

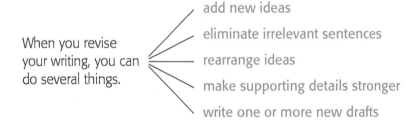

When you revise your writing, you can do several things.

- add new ideas
- eliminate irrelevant sentences
- rearrange ideas
- make supporting details stronger
- write one or more new drafts

Remember that it is almost impossible to write a perfect paragraph on your first try. That's why it is so important to read over your first draft to look for ways to improve it.

REVISING CHECKLIST FOR PARAGRAPHS	YES	NOT YET
1. Is there a clear topic sentence?		
2. Do all the sentences support the topic sentence?		
3. Is there enough information to support the topic?		
4. Are the sentences organized in a logical order?		
5. Are there transition words to guide the reader from one idea to the next?		

If the answer to any of the questions is "not yet," you need to revise that aspect of the paragraph.

As you revise a paragraph that you wrote, keep these points in mind:

- First of all, check to see if there is a clear topic sentence. If not, you need to add one.
- Then, make sure all the sentences relate to the topic stated in the topic sentence. If you find a sentence that does not relate to the topic, delete it.
- As you read, check the organization. Ask yourself if the sentences are arranged in a logical order. If they are not, you need to rearrange them.
- Have you included transitional expressions? If not, add them.
- Also, make sure you have supported the topic with enough specific evidence, such as details, facts, examples, and reasons.

Practicing Paragraph Revision

Read the following paragraphs and identify the problem(s) in each one. Use the Revising Checklist to help you. Then explain how you would revise the paragraph to make it better.

1.

My Part-time Job

Ever since I got a part-time job after school, I've had trouble managing my time. First of all, I don't have enough time to devote to my studies. I get home late, and I don't have much time to study. I have to rush through my homework, and my assignments are often late and incomplete. In addition, my social life is suffering. I never seem to have enough time to be with my friends because I'm too busy working. Some of my friends have even stopped inviting me to go out with them. Worst of all, working part-time leaves me little time for myself. I don't have time to do the things I really enjoy like reading magazines, taking pictures, and watching movies. Since I have so little time for studying, my grades are falling. Although I need the extra money I make, my job is really eating into my time.

Problem: _____

Solution: _____

2.

An Incompatible Roommate

My roommate and I are not very compatible. For one thing, we have different sleeping habits. He likes to stay up late watching TV or listening to music, but I prefer to go to bed early. In addition, he is a very neat person. He likes the room neat and clean at all times. On the other hand, I am very messy. I never hang up my clothes, and I always have books and papers scattered all over the room. Finally, while my roommate is a very social person, I am quite private. He likes to have his friends in our room and wants our room to be the party place. Luckily, we both like the same kind of music. However, I need my privacy and think of my room as my own quiet space where I can be by myself.

Problem: _____

Solution: _____

3.

Problems with Credit Cards

First of all, it is easy to spend more money than I have when I use credit cards. I often charge so much that I can't afford to pay the whole bill when it arrives. Since I can only pay a small amount each month, it's going to take me years to pay off the balance. Another problem I have with credit cards is that it's too easy to buy on impulse. I often end up purchasing things I don't really need or even like that much. I love the new pair of shoes I just charged. The interest rate on many of my cards is very high, and that's also upsetting. Some of my credit cards have a 19 percent interest rate, and the interest charges really add up! Unfortunately, I have ended up with a big debt very quickly. Therefore, I've decided to cut up my credit cards and never use them again.

Problem: _____

Solution: _____

4.   Advantages of Online College Courses

More and more students are realizing the advantages of taking college courses online or even completing entire college degrees online. Although online education, or distance learning, is not for everyone, it certainly provides a possible alternative to the traditional college experience. Why are so many students choosing to take courses online? Taking courses online offers time flexibility. For people who work or have family commitments, taking classes online is ideal. Since there is no set time for classes, you can make your own schedule, working around your other obligations. You can also work at your own pace, taking more or less time to finish a course depending on your specific needs. Distance learning is less expensive than a traditional college education. Tuition and fees are generally lower, and many of the course materials can be downloaded for free, saving you the cost of textbooks. Distance learning is convenient for people who can't or prefer not to travel to school. No matter where you live, you can take online classes if you have a computer and an Internet connection. Location is no longer an issue. If you don't live close to a college or university that offers a course or degree you want, online education offers a great opportunity. It is no wonder that the number of students benefiting from online college degrees is growing every year.

Problem: _____

Solution: _____

EDITING

After you revise your paragraph for content and organization, you still need to edit it. *Editing* means looking at each sentence carefully and correcting mistakes in grammar, spelling, and punctuation. Finding the mistakes in your paragraph is not always easy, especially if English is not your native language. However, some mistakes are very common, so you should look for them first. The following activities and examples will help you learn to correct some of the most common mistakes that students make.

Grammar Check

Look carefully at each sentence you have written and check for possible errors.

Agreement of Subjects and Verbs

You already know that every English sentence must have a subject and a verb. In order for a sentence to be grammatically correct, the subject and verb must agree with each other. This means that if the subject is singular, the verb must be singular. If the subject is plural, the verb must be plural.

Example:

*My **friend was** late for class.*

*My **friends were** late for class.*

For subject/verb agreement:

1. Find the main verb in each sentence.

2. Match the verb to its subject.

3. Make sure that the subject and verb agree in number.

Keep the following rules in mind:

- If subjects are joined by *and*, they are considered plural. Use a plural verb.

  Example:

  *My **friend** and **I were** late for class.*

- If subjects are joined by *or* or *nor*, the verb should agree with the closer subject. Use a singular verb if the subject closer to the verb is singular. Use a plural verb if the subject closer to the verb is plural.

  Examples:

  *Neither **Emily** nor **Ann plans** to join the tennis club.*

  *Neither **Ann** nor her **sisters plan** to join the tennis club.*

  In the first sentence, *Ann* is closer to the verb. Because *Ann* is singular, the verb must be singular. In the second sentence, *her sisters* is closer to the verb, so the verb must be plural.

- The verb should agree with its subject, not with the words that come between.

  Examples:

  *This new **book** of poems **is** by Pablo Neruda.*

  *The **poems** in this book **are** by Pablo Neruda.*

  The subject of the first sentence is *book*, which is singular. The subject of the second sentence is *poems*, which is plural.

- Use a singular verb with the pronouns in the chart:

SINGULAR PRONOUNS			
anyone	everybody	no one	one
anything	everyone	nobody	somebody
each	everything	none	someone
either	neither	nothing	something

Example:

***Everybody wants** to start the movie now. (Everybody is the subject.)*

- Use a plural verb with these pronouns:

PLURAL PRONOUNS				
both	few	many	others	several

Examples:

Several *of the students* ***are*** *required to write an essay.* (*Several* is the subject.)

Others ***want*** *to start the movie later.* (*Others* is the subject.)

- Use a singular verb with expressions of time, money, measurement, weight, and fractions.

Examples:

Two hours ***is*** *not enough time to study for that test.*

Twenty-five dollars ***seems*** *like a reasonable price for this sweater.*

PRACTICE **Circle the correct verb in each of the following sentences.**

1. One of my friends (has / have) a new car.

2. Everyone who works hard in this class (do / does) well.

3. Many of my friends (like / likes) the professor.

4. The instructor (don't / doesn't) give a lot of homework.

5. One of the reasons that I chose to go into medicine (is / are) that I like to work with people.

6. Fifty dollars (is / are) too much to spend on dinner at this restaurant.

7. Both Cassie and her cousin (go / goes) to the University of Michigan.

8. The book and the movie (has / have) the same ending.

Agreement of Pronouns and Nouns

Remember that a pronoun refers back to a specific noun. A pronoun should agree in number with the noun it refers to. If a pronoun refers to a singular noun, you must use a singular pronoun. If a pronoun refers to a plural noun, you must use a plural pronoun.

Examples:

When a ***student*** *eats in the cafeteria,* ***he*** *or* ***she*** *must show a student ID.*

When ***students*** *eat in the cafeteria,* ***they*** *must show a student ID.*

For pronoun/noun agreement:

1. Read over your paper, stopping at each pronoun.

2. Identify the noun that the pronoun replaces. Make sure it agrees with the pronoun. If you can't find the noun, you must add one or change the pronoun to a noun.

As you saw earlier, the following pronouns are singular. Use a singular verb for these pronouns:

SINGULAR PRONOUNS			
anyone	everybody	no one	one
anything	everyone	nobody	somebody
each	everything	none	someone
either	neither	nothing	something

PRACTICE **Circle the correct verb in each of the following sentences.**

1. Everyone on the team (comes / come) to practice every day.

2. All the team members (has / have) to work hard.

3. Each one of your students (is / are) improving.

4. He said, "Nobody (cares / care) about the game."

5. Someone (is / are) going to pay for this mistake.

Clear Pronoun Reference

Good writers use pronouns to avoid repeating a noun in a sentence or paragraph. Make sure that every pronoun you use refers clearly to one specific noun. This noun is called the **antecedent**.

Example:

After Pam ironed the dress, she put it in her suitcase.

In this sentence, *it* clearly refers to the dress.

When a pronoun does not have a clear antecedent, the reader can be easily confused.

Example:

After Pam ironed the dress and the jacket, she put it in the suitcase.

In this sentence, the pronoun *it* does not have a clear antecedent. It could refer to the dress or the jacket.

When a pronoun reference is unclear, you can correct the sentence by using the specific noun.

Example:

After Pam ironed the dress and the jacket, she put the dress in the suitcase and decided to wear the jacket.

PRACTICE **Correct the sentences so that each pronoun refers to a specific noun.**

1. After the coach gave Tim the ball, he walked onto the soccer field.

2. When Yoko saw her sister, she smiled.

3. Justin told his father that he should take a taxi.

4. Harriet told Nancy that she had made a big mistake.

5. Luke and Dave went to the new Japanese restaurant, but he forgot his wallet.

6. My kite hit the window, but luckily it was not broken.

Agreement of Possessive Pronouns and Adjectives

Pay special attention to possessive forms. Just as a pronoun and the noun it refers to must agree, a possessive must agree with the word it refers to. If the word referred to is singular, the possessive adjective or pronoun must be singular. If the word is plural, the possessive adjective or pronoun must be plural.

Examples:

*The little **boy** is holding **his** mother's hand.*

*The **children** are holding **their** mothers' hands.*

***Each** of the girls had **her** own bedroom in the apartment.*

***Both** of our daughters have **their** own cars.*

*Give it to **Jane**. It's **hers**.*

*That book belongs to **me**. It's **mine**.*

PRACTICE **Circle the correct possessive in each of these sentences.**

1. Both of the students forgot (his / their) notebooks.

2. Neither of my sisters owns (her / their) own house.

3. Matthew likes (his / their) meat cooked well done.

4. The Wexlers send (his / their) children to private school.

5. One of the women has retired from (her / their) job.

6. This isn't Wendy's jacket. It's (my / mine).

7. Allie bought that iPod from me, so now it's (hers / her's).

Avoiding Sentence Fragments

An English sentence must have a subject and a verb. It must also express a complete thought. A complete sentence can stand alone. That is, it makes sense by itself. If a sentence lacks either a subject or a verb or if it is not a complete thought, it is called a *sentence fragment*.

There are three main kinds of fragments:

1. No subject

   Fragment: Did very well on her math exam.

   Complete Sentence: *Georgette* did very well on her math exam.

2. No verb

Fragment: Both Alexander and his younger sister Lisa.

Complete Sentence: Both Alexander and his younger sister Lisa *enjoy* tennis.

3. No independent clause/not a complete thought

Fragment: Before I went to college.

Complete Sentence: Before I went to college, *I worked part-time at a bank.*

A dependent clause is often confused with a complete sentence because it contains a subject and a verb. However, it is not a complete thought. A dependent clause must be attached to an independent clause to form a complete sentence with a complete thought. These words are often used to begin dependent clauses. They are called *subordinating conjunctions.*

SUBORDINATING CONJUNCTIONS			
after	even if	though	where
although	even though	unless	wherever
as	if	until	which
because	since	whatever	while
before	so that	when	who
despite	that	whenever	whose

Example:

Because the meteorologist predicted rain.

Although this clause has a subject and verb, it is not a complete sentence. It does not make sense by itself.

There are two possible ways to correct this mistake:

1. Make the dependent clause a complete sentence by removing the word *Because*.

Sentence fragment: Because the meteorologist predicted rain.

Complete sentence: The meteorologist predicted rain.

2. Attach the dependent clause to an independent clause.

Sentence fragment: Because the meteorologist predicted rain.

Complete sentence: Because the meteorologist predicted rain, *I took my umbrella with me.*

PRACTICE **A** **Write *C* in front of each *complete sentence*. Write *F* in front of each *sentence fragment*. Then rewrite the fragments so that they are complete sentences.**

    F   **1.** Works out in the gym every day.

               My father works out in the gym every day.

        2. I love visiting Monet's gardens in Giverny because gardening is my hobby.

        3. Hockey can be a very dangerous sport if you don't have the right equipment.

        4. Because I couldn't understand the homework.

        5. And ran out of gas on the way to work.

        6. Whenever my next-door neighbor has time.

        7. Although she had a bad cold and hadn't slept well for days.

        8. That my friend told me was the best movie he had ever seen.

B **Write a sentence using each of the following words.**

    1. after

    2. although

    3. because

    4. before

5. if

_____

6. since

_____

7. unless

_____

8. when

_____

9. until

_____

10. despite

_____

C **Exchange sentences with a classmate. Check your partner's sentences. Are they all complete sentences?**

Avoiding Run-on Sentences and Comma Splices

Run-on sentences occur when two complete sentences are written as one sentence. One kind of run-on sentence is a comma splice. This happens when two related complete sentences are joined with a comma.

Run-on example: Judy is celebrating she won first prize.

Comma splice example: Luis is tired, he is going to sleep early tonight.

There are three ways to correct run-on sentences:

1. Use punctuation, usually a period, to separate the two sentences.

Run-on sentence: Sue loves to cook she is always in the kitchen.

Correct sentences: Sue loves to cook. _She_ is always in the kitchen.

2. Use a comma plus coordinating conjunction (_and, but, however, for, so, or, nor, yet_) to connect the two clauses.

Run-on sentence: The movie was boring we watched it anyway.

Correct sentence: The movie was boring, _but_ we watched it anyway.

3. Use a subordinating conjunction to connect the two clauses.

Run-on sentence: I'm very hungry I didn't eat breakfast.

Correct sentence: I'm very hungry *because* I didn't eat breakfast.

PRACTICE **Write *C* in front of each *complete sentence*. Write *R* in front of each *run-on sentence*. Then correct the run-on sentences.**

_____ **1.** I like my dentist he is very gentle.

_____

_____ **2.** My son bought two T-shirts he thought they were so cool.

_____

_____ **3.** It was too cold yesterday to ski we stayed in the lodge all day.

_____

_____ **4.** When Jerry finishes work, he'll join us at the party.

_____

_____ **5.** The Pilgrims first came to Plymouth, Massachusetts, in 1620 they were seeking religious freedom.

_____

_____ **6.** If all twenty-five of us agree, it will be a miracle.

_____

_____ **7.** Dennis called to say that his computer is making strange noises he thinks it is broken.

_____

_____ **8.** They wanted to play golf but we thought it was too hot we all went swimming instead.

_____

_____ **9.** There are several ways to get from New York to Philadelphia the most convenient is by train.

_____

_____ **10.** I have a very good memory my husband, on the other hand, does not.

_____

Gerunds and Infinitives

Gerunds

A gerund is a verb form that can be used as a noun. Gerunds are formed by adding *-ing* to the base form of a verb. Gerunds can be used as subject, objects, or complements of a sentence.

Examples:

Reading helps build your vocabulary. (*Reading* is the subject of the sentence.)

Lee's hobby is reading. (*Reading* is the complement of the sentence.)

He enjoys reading. (*Reading* is the object of the sentence.)

Infinitives

Infinitives are also a verb form that can be used as a noun. Infinitives are the "to" form of the verb. The infinitive form of *read* is *to read*. Infinitives are often used as the object of a sentence.

Example:

She wants to read. (*To read* is the object of the sentence.)

Gerunds and infinitives can both function as the subject, but gerunds are much more common.

More common: *Reading is important.*

Less common: *To read is important.*

Gerunds and infinitives can both function as the object of a sentence. The main verb in the sentence determines whether you use a gerund or an infinitive.

Examples:

He enjoys making new friends. (*Enjoy* requires a gerund.)

He wants to make new friends. (*Want* requires an infinitive.)

These common verbs can be followed by gerunds as objects.

avoid	I **avoid** drinking coffee in the evening.
enjoy	He **enjoys** swimming.
finish	She **finished** revising her essay.
quit	I **quit** smoking last year.
miss	I **miss** living in a big city.
practice	The little boy **practices** riding a bike after school.
keep	She **keeps** looking at the clock.

These common verbs can be followed by infinitives as objects.

decide	We **decided** to take a taxi to the restaurant.
want	I **want** to learn Korean.
hope	They **hope** to finish the project today.
need	I **need** to study for the exam.
plan	We **plan** to take a vacation this summer.
promise	I **promise** to text you when I get home.
agree	He **agreed** to work on Saturday.

These common verbs can be followed by gerunds or infinitives. The meaning of the sentence does not change whether you use the gerund or the infinitive.

begin	I **began** studying Arabic in college.	I **began** to study Arabic in college.
like	She **likes** baking.	She **likes** to bake.
hate	My sister **hates** flying.	My sister **hates** to fly.
start	I **started** studying after dinner.	I **started** to study after dinner.
love	I **love** surfing.	I **love** to surf.
prefer	They **prefer** to walk to work.	They **prefer** walking to work.

PRACTICE **Correct the eight sentences in this list that have mistakes in gerunds and infinitives.**

1. Victoria enjoys to work with small children.

2. I decided taking another economics course.

3. I promise to do my homework as soon as I get home.

4. Jason keeps to look at his watch. I think he is bored.

5. They prefer live in the suburbs.

6. She agreed helping me with the assignment.

7. He finished to study at 9:00.

8. Janet likes getting up early.

9. They decided moving to a bigger apartment.

10. I hope completing my degree in four years.

Despite an intensive search, no one at the party was able to find Marcy's misplaced semicolon.

Using Parallel Structures

Parts of a sentence that have the same function should also have the same grammatical construction. The parts of a sentence include words, phrases, and clauses. These parts should be in the same grammatical form so that they are *parallel*.

Here are three rules about parallel structure that will help you when you are editing your writing.

1. Use parallel structure when parts of a sentence are joined by coordinating conjunctions: *and*, *but*, *for*, *or*, *nor*, *yet*, *so*.

    Incorrect: You need to work quickly and be quiet.

    Correct: You need to work quickly and quietly.

    Incorrect: We need to reduce spending or raising taxes.

    Correct: We need to reduce spending or raise taxes.

2. Use parallel structure for items in a list or a series:

    Incorrect: I like movies that have good actors, interesting plots, and endings that surprise me.

    Correct: I like movies that have good actors, interesting plots, and surprise endings.

    Incorrect: I use my cell phone to call people, texting my friends, take pictures, and check my email.

    Correct: I use my cell phone to call people, text my friends, take pictures, and check my email.

3. Use parallel Structure when you compare or contrast parts of a sentence. (X is better than Y, or X is less than Y):

    Incorrect: Carol enjoys reading more than to write.

    Correct: Carol enjoys reading more than writing.

Incorrect: It costs less to take the subway than taking a taxi.

Correct: It costs less to take the subway than to take a taxi.

PRACTICE **Ⓐ** **Write *P* in front of each sentence that is parallel. Write *NP* in front of each sentence that is not parallel. Then correct the sentences that are not parallel on a separate piece of paper.**

_____ 1. I spent the morning doing laundry, dusting furniture, and washing dishes.

_____ 2. I'm going to vote for Nathan because he is honest, intelligent and works hard.

_____ 3. She read the instructions slowly and with care.

_____ 4. Taking the train is fast, comfortable, and safe.

_____ 5. You can vote by calling, texting or send an email.

_____ 6. Tom likes riding his bike more than to take a taxi.

_____ 7. Jogging and to swim are good exercise.

_____ 8. Paula is honest and you can rely on her.

_____ 9. We enjoy visiting our friends more than staying home.

_____ 10. You can do the activity individually, in pairs, or work with four people in a group.

_____ 11. Her new dress is beautiful but it cost a lot.

_____ 12. The movie was long, boring, and it depressed me.

Ⓑ **Circle the correct word or phrase that gives the sentence parallel structure.**

1. Taking the train is fast, convenient, and _____.

    a. economical

    b. doesn't cost a lot of money

    c. reasonably priced

2. I enjoyed reading the book more than _____.

    a. I watched the movie

    b. watching the movie

    c. to watch the movie

3. When the weather is sunny and _____, I like to be outdoors.

   a. starting to get warm

   b. warm

   c. getting warm

4. Reading, cooking, and _____ are three of Lisa's favorite hobbies.

   a. knitting

   b. to knit

   c. learn to knit

5. She spends her time studying English, working at the library, and _____.

   a. she watches television

   b. watching television

   c. in front of the television

Using Correct Punctuation and Capitalization

Punctuation

Punctuation marks, such as commas, periods, and quotation marks, help readers interpret sentences. They determine how a sentence should be read and understood. Like most languages, English has certain rules of punctuation. The following guidelines will help you master some of the most important ones.

Period

• Use a period at the end of a statement:

   Argentina's economy is a mix of agriculture and industry.

• Use a period with most abbreviations:

   Mr.   A.M.   apt.   St.   Tues.   M.D.

   Mrs.   P.M.   Ave.   Aug.   Dr.

Question Mark

• Use a question mark at the end of a question:

   Who is going to drive me to the airport?

Comma

- Use a comma to separate words or phrases in a series:

    The sea around Antarctica is home to *dolphins, porpoises, whales, seals,* and *other sea creatures*.

- Use a comma to separate independent clauses joined by a coordinating conjunction:

    We left in plenty of time, *but* we still missed the bus.

    I worked hard all day, *so* I went to bed early.

- Use a comma after many introductory phrases or dependent clauses:

    Working late into the night, I drank several cups of strong coffee.

    Because I was tired, I went to sleep early last night.

- Use a comma before a direct quote:

    Christina said, *"The train leaves in half an hour."*

- Use a comma between the day of the month and the year:

    August 15, 1983

- Use a comma to separate cities from states:

    Billings, Montana

    Tallahassee, Florida

Colon

- Use a colon to introduce a series:

    The museum offers daily tours of the following collections: *American, Asian, Classical, European, and Contemporary art.*

- Use a colon to introduce a long or formal quotation:

    Writing about his life, British philosopher Bertrand Russell said: *"Three passions, simple but overwhelmingly strong, have governed my life: the longing for love, the search for knowledge, and the unbearable pity for the suffering of mankind."*

    Note: The first colon is used to introduce the quotation; the second one introduces a series.

- Use a colon to separate hours from minutes:

    3:15

    6:45

- Use a colon after the salutation in a formal letter:

    Dear Dr. Brody:

    Dear Ms. Rosen:

Semicolon

- Use a semicolon to combine two very closely related complete sentences.

    Lin is saving his money; he wants to buy a new car.

    I drank too much coffee after dinner; I can't fall asleep.

    I brought an umbrella; it is supposed to rain this afternoon.

- Use a semicolon with a conjunctive adverb and a comma to clarify the relationship between two closely related complete sentences. The most common conjunctive adverbs include *however, therefore, in addition, moreover, subsequently, consequently, instead,* and *additionally.*

    Young-Hee passed the English test; however, she still wants to take one more English class.

    Patrick works hard all week; therefore, he likes to relax on the weekends.

Quotation Marks

- Use quotation marks to enclose a direct quote:

    Jorge said, *"I have already finished my homework."*

- Use quotation marks to identify titles of songs, short stories, poems, articles, essays, and chapters from a book. Underline the titles of longer works such as books and newspapers. Underline the titles of paintings and other works of art. (If you are using a computer, the titles of longer works and art should be in italic type instead of underlined.)

    My favorite song is *"Imagine"* by John Lennon.

    One of Andrew Wyeth's best-known paintings is *Christina's World.*

PRACTICE **Punctuate the following sentences.**

1. He was born in Portland on April 22 1981

2. How many books have you read lately

3. We will have to leave by 530 PM

4. Dr Anderson has a very full schedule today

5. I just finished reading Hemingway's novel The Old Man and the Sea

6. Most people like chocolate but Jane is allergic to it

7. I woke up with a headache therefore I decided not to go to class this morning

8. The restaurant has three specialties grilled steak marinated chicken and fried shrimp

9. In conclusion Mario Vargas Llosa is one of the greatest writers of the twentieth century

10. Marion said I can't go with you because I have too much homework

11. I think that Pablo Neruda's poem If You Forget Me is the most beautiful poem I've ever read

12. I like to watch science fiction movies however I don't like to read science fiction novels.

Capitalization

The following rules summarize the main uses of capitalization in English. If you are not sure when to capitalize a word, you should use your dictionary as a reference.

- Capitalize the first word of a sentence:

  Fishing is an important industry in Peru.

- Capitalize names. Capitalize a title that precedes a name:

  Dr. Lourie
  Professor Cantor
  David

- Capitalize the names of racial and ethnic groups:

  African American
  Asian
  Caucasian

  Exception: Do not capitalize the words *black* or *white* when referring to racial groups.

- Capitalize the names of specific geographical locations including countries, states, cities, towns, rivers, streets, and mountains:

  Paris
  Juniper Avenue
  Mount Rushmore

- Capitalize the days of the week, months, and holidays:

  Tuesday
  September
  Christmas, New Year's Eve, Ramadan, Thanksgiving

- Capitalize the names of religions:

  Buddhism
  Christianity
  Islam

- Capitalize nationalities and languages:

  Japanese
  Arabic

- Capitalize all words in a title except articles, prepositions, and conjunctions, unless they are the first or the last word in the title:

  "Give Peace a Chance"
  The Curious Case of Benjamin Button
  Ready to Write

PRACTICE Capitalize each of the following sentences correctly.

1. my russian teacher is very handsome.

2. have you read *romeo and juliet* in your english literature class yet?

3. i meet with my advisor every tuesday and thursday morning.

4. my sister, ruth, has just returned from a trip to istanbul and athens.

5. shopping is one of the most popular activities of visitors to new york city.

6. we usually celebrate thanksgiving with our cousins, betty and alvin.

Punctuation and Capitalization Review

Add the correct capitalization and punctuation to the sentences that follow.

1. traffic is causing serious pollution in some cities such as athens mexico city and los angeles

2. when will professor klein be in his office

3. my favorite poem is fire and ice by robert frost

4. i'll meet you on tuesday afternoon at 430 in front of the library on liberty street

5. mrs baker is one of the most inspiring speakers i've ever heard

6. the earliest maps anyone knows of were made by babylonians and egyptians more than 4,000 years ago

7. the himalayas are the world's highest mountains

8. maria asked what time does the movie casablanca start

9. in 1980 the wildlife biologist george shaller began researching the panda in its natural habitat

10. professor dickens is sick so his tuesday night class will be canceled

Commonly Confused Words

Ⓐ **Learn the differences in meaning for these commonly confused words:**

WORDS/ PHRASES	MEANING/ USAGE	EXAMPLES
accept except	Verb, meaning "to take willingly" Preposition, meaning "to exclude"	I *accept* your apology. I ate everything *except* the dessert.
advice advise	Noun, meaning "a recommendation" Verb, meaning "to give advice"	Please take my *advice*. I *advise* you to study hard.
affect effect	Verb, meaning "to influence" Noun, meaning "a change that is a result of something"	What factors will *affect* your decision? My father had a big *effect* on my life.
it's its	Contraction of *it is* Possessive adjective	*It's* time to leave. The school changed *its* admission policy.

WORDS/ PHRASES	MEANING/ USAGE	EXAMPLES
loose	Adjective, meaning the "opposite of tight"	These pants are too *loose*. I need a smaller size.
lose	Verb, meaning "to misplace"	Try not to *lose* the keys to my apartment.
quite	Adverb of degree, meaning "very" or "rather"	I'm *quite* hungry.
quiet	Adjective, meaning "the opposite of noisy"	Please be *quiet* during the exam.
right	Adjective, meaning "correct" or "proper"	You made the *right* decision.
write	Verb, meaning "to put words on paper"	*Write* your name here.
suppose	Verb, meaning "to think" or "to guess"	I *suppose* it belongs to him.
be supposed to	Verb phrase, meaning "should"	He *is supposed to* take this medicine now.
than	Conjunction, used to show comparison	My car is older *than* yours.
then	Adverb, meaning "after that"	We ate lunch. *Then* we took a nap.
their	Possessive form of *they*	Tina and Lewis love *their* new car.
there	Adverb, shows location	Put the book over *there*.
they're	Contraction of *they are*	*They're* late for class again.
to	Preposition, meaning "toward"	I am going *to* the library.
too	Adverb, meaning "also" or "very"	Marsha is going, *too*. This soup is *too* hot. Don't eat it yet.
two	The number 2	Gail has *two* brothers.
use	Verb, meaning "to utilize"	I *use* sugar in my coffee.
used	Past form of *use*	He *used* all the soap.
be used to	Verb phrase, meaning "be accustomed to"	I *am used to* getting up early.
weather	Noun referring to the temperature and other conditions such as sun, rain, and wind	The *weather* is nice in Istanbul in the spring.
whether	Used when talking about a choice you have to make or about something that is not certain	I don't know *whether* or not to wear a heavy coat today.
whose	Possessive form of *who*	*Whose* book is this?
who's	Contraction of *who is*	*Who's* singing that song?
your	Possessive form of *you*	*Your* dress is very pretty.
you're	Contraction of *you are*	*You're* late for the meeting.

B Work with a partner to write a sentence for each of the commonly confused words on the list. Then exchange papers with another pair and read each other's sentences. Do you see any mistakes? Correct the sentences where you find mistakes.

> **WRITER'S TIP:** Spelling
>
> If you are writing on a computer, do not rely solely on the spell check tool. It will not catch every mistake. Look at each word you wrote separately by reading your paper very carefully. If you are not sure how to spell a word, check a dictionary.

Spelling Check

When you are editing your writing, you should check for spelling errors. If you are not sure how to spell a word, look it up in a dictionary. English spelling can be confusing because it is so inconsistent. Here are some rules that you can practice and learn to help you improve your spelling.

SPELLING RULES FOR THE PLURAL OF NOUNS		
Nouns	**Plural**	**Examples**
Most nouns	Add *-s*	car, car*s*; lamp, lamp*s*; house, house*s*
Most nouns that end in *-ch, -sh, -s, -x,* or *-z*	Add *-es*	fox, fox*es*; bus, bus*es*; brush, brush*es*
Most nouns that end in a vowel and *-y*	Add *-s*	toy, toy*s*; tray, tray*s*; day, day*s*
Most nouns that end in a consonant and *-y*	*y* becomes *ies*	baby, bab*ies*; country, countr*ies*; spy, sp*ies*
Most nouns that end in *-f* or *-fe*	*f* or *fe* becomes *ves*	shelf, shel*ves*; wife, wi*ves*; half, hal*ves*
Most nouns that end in *-o*	Add *-s*	radio, radio*s*; studio, studio*s*; video, video*s*
Certain nouns that end in a consonant and *-o*	Add *-es*	hero, hero*es*; echo, echo*es*; potato, potato*es*

SPELLING RULES FOR SIMPLE PRESENT SINGULAR VERBS WITH *HE, SHE,* AND *IT*		
Verb	**Simple Present Singular Verbs with *he, she,* and *it***	**Examples**
For most verbs	Add the letter *-s* to the base form of the verb	speak*s*, listen*s*, run*s*, help*s*
For verbs that end in *-sh, -ch, -ss, -x*	Add *-es*	push*es*, watch*es*, kiss*es*
For verbs that end in a consonant + *y*	Change *y* to *i* and then add *-es*	tr*ies*, dr*ies*, worr*ies*

SPELLING RULES FOR ADDING *-ING*		
Verb	**Adding *-ing***	**Examples**
For most verbs	Add *-ing* to the base form of the verb	sing, sing***ing***; walk, walk***ing***; do, do***ing***
For verbs that end in *-e*	Drop the final *-e* and add *-ing*	make, mak***ing***; state, stat***ing***; leave, leav***ing***
For most verbs that end in consonant-vowel-consonant combination (CVC)	Double the last consonant and then add *-ing*	hit, hit***ting***; begin, begin***ning***; stop, stop***ping***
For verbs that end in *-ie*	Change the *-ie*, to *-y*, then add *-ing*	lie, l***ying***; tie, t***ying***

Exceptions:

1. Do <u>not</u> double the last consonant in verbs that end in *-w*, *-x*, or *-y*.

    Examples: *sew, sewing; fix, fixing; enjoy, enjoying*

2. Do not double the last consonant if the last syllable of a verb is not stressed.

    Examples: *happen, happening; listen, listening*

SPELLING RULES FOR ADDING *-ED* TO REGULAR VERBS		
Verb	**Adding *-ed***	**Examples**
For most verbs	Add *-ed* to the base form of the verb	talk, talk***ed***; discuss, discuss***ed***; walk, walk***ed***
For verbs that end in *-e*	Add *-d*	note, not***ed***; save, sav***ed***; invite, invite***d***
For most verbs that end in consonant-vowel-consonant combination (CVC)	Double the last consonant and then add *-ed*	stop, stop***ped***; plan; plan***ned***; beg, beg***ged***
For verbs that end in consonant + *y*	Drop the *y* and add *-ied*	reply, repl***ied***; study, stud***ied***; apply, appl***ied***

Exceptions:

1. Do <u>not</u> double the last consonant in verbs that end in *-w*, *-x*, or *-y*.

    Examples: *sew, sewed; fix, fixed; enjoy, enjoyed*

2. Do not double the last consonant if the last syllable of a verb is not stressed.

    Examples: *listen, listened; develop, developed*

PRACTICE **Complete each sentence with the word in parentheses plus the ending. Make other necessary changes.**

1. (plan + -*ed*) We _____ to play tennis, but it rained all afternoon.

2. (bounce + -*ing*) The little boy is _____ his new ball.

3. (supply + -*s*) The owner of the apartment _____ the paint.

4. (knife + -*s*) These _____ are very sharp. Keep them away from the children.

5. (begin + -*ing*) The movie is _____ soon.

6. (mix + -*ing*) She is _____ the butter and sugar together.

7. (damage + -*ed*) The storm _____ many buildings.

8. (watch + -*s*) My neighbor _____ my daughter when I have to work late.

9. (enjoy + -*ed*) We really _____ the party.

10. (lie + -*ing*) I'm not sure if he is telling the truth or _____.

EDITING CHECKLIST FOR PARAGRAPHS AND ESSAYS	YES	NOT YET
1. Is the first sentence of each paragraph indented?		
2. Do your subjects and verbs agree?		
3. Do your nouns, pronouns, and possessives agree?		
4. Are all the sentences complete (no fragments)?		
5. Have you eliminated run-on sentences?		
6. Is the punctuation correct in all the sentences?		
7. Does the first word of each sentence begin with a capital letter?		
8. Are all your words spelled correctly?		
9. Do all your pronouns have clear antecedents?		
10. Are gerunds and infinitives used correctly?		

C **If the answer to any of the questions is "not yet," go back and try to improve your paragraph.**

PUTTING IT ALL TOGETHER

You are going to write an article for the travel section of a newspaper. The focus of your article will be how to plan a trip that will be economical, educational, and fun.

 Prewriting

A **It is often easier to write after you have talked about the subject with some other people. In small groups, discuss ways to make travel economical, educational, and fun. Write the ideas that your group discusses in the chart.**

ECONOMICAL	EDUCATIONAL	FUN

B **Now complete the following steps as you draft your article.**

1. Group the items on the list that go together.

2. Cross out items that do not belong.

3. On a separate piece of paper, make a simple outline of your paragraph.

 Writing

On a separate piece of paper, write the first draft of your article.

Revising and Editing

A **Work with a partner. Ask your partner to read the first draft of your article and to make suggestions about how to revise it. Your partner should use the Revising Checklist on page 52.**

B **Edit your article for grammar, spelling, and punctuation errors. Use the Editing Checklist on page 75 as a guide. Make a final copy of your article and give it to your teacher.**

YOU BE THE EDITOR

The paragraph below has twelve mistakes. Correct the mistakes and copy the revised paragraph on a separate piece of paper.

There are a lot of interesting things to see and do in new york city. It is home to more than 150 world-class museums. Their are art museums, science museums, photography museums, natural history museums, and even a museum of seaport history. New York is known for their rich variety of theater, music, and dance. From the bright lights of Broadway and the respected stages at Lincoln Center and Carnegie Hall to the high kicks of the Rockettes at Radio City Music Hall and incredible jazz at intimate clubs, there is something for everyone. Many people go to New York. For the wonderful restaurants. There are thousands of restaurants to please every palate and wallet If you are looking for a place to shop. You will find everything you can imagine. With more than 10,000 shops filled with brand names and bargains from around the world, NYC are a shopper's paradise. as for me, people-watching is my favorite New York pastime.

CHAPTER HIGHLIGHTS

Complete the paragraph below by filling in the blanks. You do not have to use exact words from the chapter as long as the ideas are correct.

The last step in the writing process involves _____ and

_____. When you revise something you wrote, you should look
        2.

for ways you can _____ it. When you revise your writing, you can
                       3.

_____ _____,
        4.   **5.**

and _____. First of all, make sure there is a clear
          6.

_____. Then check to see if all the supporting sentences
          7.

_____ to the topic. If you find a sentence that does not relate
          8.

to the topic, _____ 9. _____ it. As you read, check the organization. Ask

yourself if the sentences are arranged in a _____ 10. _____. Be sure you

have included _____ 11. _____ to guide the reader from one idea to the

next. It is also important to revise your writing so that you have supported the topic with specific

evidence such as _____ 12. _____, _____ 13. _____,

_____ 14. _____, and _____ 15. _____.

Finally, when you edit your writing, you correct the _____ 16. _____,

_____ 17. _____, and _____ 18. _____.

CHAPTER 4 ▸ Writing Essays

....
LEARNING OUTCOME
....
Essay Writing: Write a five-paragraph essay about a preference such as living in a small town or living in a big city

Learning to write an essay builds on many of the skills you have already mastered in learning to write a paragraph. Once you know how to write a paragraph, it is not much harder to write an essay; an essay is just longer.

Basically, an essay is a group of paragraphs about a specific subject. Like a paragraph, an essay makes and supports one main point. However, the subject of an essay is too complex to be developed in a few sentences. Several paragraphs are needed to fully support the main point of an essay. A typical essay has five paragraphs, but many other types of essays are longer or shorter, depending on their purpose. In this book, you will learn the basic formula for a five-paragraph essay.

PARTS OF AN ESSAY

A basic essay has three main parts: an *introduction*, a *body* (several *supporting paragraphs*), and a *conclusion*. Each part has its own special purpose. The introduction provides some background information on the subject and states the main idea in a thesis statement. The supporting paragraphs (often called the body) explain and support the main idea with examples, details, reasons, and facts. The conclusion summarizes the main points.

BASIC PLAN OF A FIVE-PARAGRAPH ESSAY

Introduction (1 paragraph)

- Gives background information or an overview of the subject
- Gets reader's attention
- Ends with a thesis statement that states the subject and focus of the essay

Body Paragraph 1

Topic Sentence: States first supporting point
Supporting Sentences: Provide supporting details, examples, facts

Body Paragraph 2

Topic Sentence: States second supporting point
Supporting Sentences: Provide supporting details, examples, facts

Body Paragraph 3

Topic Sentence: States third supporting point
Supporting Sentences: Provide supporting details, examples, facts

Conclusion (1 paragraph)

- Makes final comments about the subject
- Restates main points
- Leaves reader with something to think about

WRITER'S TIP: Organizing Essays

Although some essays do not fit into the five-paragraph format, most essays follow some pattern of organization. The format is simply a plan to help you arrange your ideas into a systematic order. Most essays have a recognizable beginning, middle, and end.

If you know how to write a basic five-paragraph essay, you will always have something to fall back on.

Read the essay and label the parts on the lines provided.

Accidental Inventions

Many inventions happen when someone is looking for a faster, easier, or better way of doing something. They are the result of years of planning and hard work. But not all of them started out like that. Lots of inventions happened because of an accident someone had or a mistake someone made. For example, did you know that ice cream cones, blue jeans, chocolate chip cookies, and Velcro are all the result of accidents? Some people have saved millions of lives because of an accident they had. Others have become rich by turning their accident into big business. Three of the most well-known inventions or discoveries that happened by accident are popsicles, microwave ovens, and penicillin.

_____

Popsicles were invented by accident by an eleven-year-old boy named Frank Epperson. In 1905, Frank accidentally left his fruit-flavored drink outside on the porch with a stir stick in it. During the night, it became very cold outside. Frank's drink froze with the wooden stick still in it. The next day Frank tasted the frozen drink. It was delicious. Eighteen years later, in 1923, Frank Epperson remembered his frozen drink. He decided to start a business making and selling the frozen drinks. He called them Epsicles, and he made them in seven fruit flavors. The name was later changed to the Popsicle. The next time you eat a popsicle on a hot summer day, remember that it was invented by accident.

_____

Like popsicles, microwave ovens were an accidental discovery. Many people use microwave ovens because they cook food much faster than regular ovens. The first microwave oven wasn't invented because someone was trying to find a faster way to cook food. The idea of cooking food using microwave energy was discovered by accident. In 1946, an engineer named Dr. Percy LeBaron Spencer was researching microwaves. As he was working, he noticed that the chocolate candy in his pocket had melted. He guessed that the microwaves had caused the chocolate to melt. He decided to see what would happen if he put other kinds of food, such as popcorn and eggs, near the microwaves. He discovered that the popcorn popped and the eggs cooked. Spencer soon realized that microwaves cooked food very quickly. In fact, microwaves cooked foods even faster than heat. Dr. Spencer had discovered, by accident, a process that changed cooking forever. He went on to build the first microwave oven, which began a multimillion-dollar industry.

_____

Finally, while popsicles are good to eat and microwave ovens make cooking faster and easier, one accidental discovery, penicillin, has saved millions of lives since its discovery in 1928. No one planned to discover penicillin. It happened by accident when a British doctor named Alexander Fleming was doing research on bacteria. One day Fleming was cleaning up his laboratory, and he noticed that a green mold was growing next to the bacteria. He looked at the mold under a microscope. He was surprised to find that the mold had killed some of the bacteria. Fleming thought the mold might be able to kill bacteria inside our bodies that cause many diseases. He was right, and soon the mold was developed into penicillin. Fleming said, "I did not invent penicillin. Nature did that. I only discovered it by accident." Today we realize that the discovery of penicillin was one of the most important events in the history of medicine.

_____

So, if you ever feel bad because you made a mistake, just remember that some of the most important inventions in the world were discovered by accident. Popsicles, microwave ovens, and penicillin are just three of the many discoveries that were not planned. They all happened by accident.

Alexander Fleming in his laboratory in 1928, where he first saw the penicillin mold.

The Introduction

The *introduction* is the first paragraph of your essay. It should capture the readers' attention and make them want to read the rest of the essay. The introduction should start with some general statements about your subject and lead up to a specific statement of your main idea, or thesis.

The format of an introductory paragraph is different from the format of most other kinds of paragraphs. In introductory paragraphs, the main idea is usually stated in the *last* sentence. This sentence is called the *thesis statement*.

WRITER'S TIP: Introductions

The function of the introduction is:

- to capture the reader's interest;
- to provide background information; and
- to state the main idea of the essay in a thesis statement.

There are no specific rules for writing an introduction, but there are several techniques. Many introductions use one or a combination of the following techniques to provide background information and capture the reader's attention.

- **Move from general to specific.**

  This type of introduction opens with a general statement on the subject that establishes its importance and then leads the reader to the more specific thesis statement.

- **Use an anecdote.**

  Another way to write an introduction is to relate an interesting story that will interest the reader in the subject. Newspaper and magazine writers frequently use this technique to begin their articles.

- **Use a quotation.**

  A quotation is an easy way to introduce your topic. You can quote an authority on your subject or use an interesting quotation from an article. You can also be more informal and use a proverb or favorite saying of a friend or relative.

- **Ask a question.**

  Asking one or more questions at the beginning of an essay is a good way to engage readers in the topic right away. They will want to read on in order to find the answers to the questions.

- **Present facts and statistics.**

  Presenting some interesting facts or statistics establishes credibility.

PRACTICE **A** Reread the introduction for the essay "Accidental Inventions" on page 81. Notice that the student begins with a general statement about inventions and then moves to a more specific statement about them.

B Read these sample introductions. In small groups, identify the technique or techniques used in each one. Remember that authors often use a combination of techniques to write an introduction.

1.   Karate, which literally means "the art of empty hands," is the most widely practiced of all the martial arts. It is primarily a means of self-defense that uses the body as a weapon for striking, kicking, and blocking. Having originated in the ancient Orient, the art of karate is more than 1,000 years old. It developed first as a form of monastic training and later became a method of self-defense. During the seventeenth century, karate became highly developed as an art on the Japanese island of Okinawa. Over the years, this ancient art has gained much popularity, and today karate is practiced throughout the world. More than a method of combat, karate emphasizes self-discipline, positive attitude, and high moral purpose.

   Technique(s): _____

   _____

**These two office workers share a job and
meet occasionally to compare notes.**

2.   It is often said that "Two heads are better than one." For the past two years, the job of research assistant in my office has been shared very successfully by two people. This "job-sharing" arrangement has worked out quite well for all involved. Throughout the business world, the interest in flexible employment arrangements, such as job-sharing, is growing. Employers are beginning to realize that there are many talented people out there who are looking for alternatives to traditional patterns of employment. In a job-sharing arrangement, a full-time job is shared by two people. As an executive in a multinational firm, I feel that job-sharing is not only helpful to employees but also offers several advantages to employers. A job-sharing arrangement increases productivity, helps maintain diversity, and brings a broader range of skills to the job.

Technique(s): _____

_____

3.   Homicide is the cause of death for more children in Washington, D.C., than any other single cause involving injury, including car accidents, house fires, and drowning. Unfortunately, this phenomenon is not exclusive to Washington. The overcrowded neighborhoods of many big U.S. cities, such as Detroit, Dallas, St. Louis, Atlanta, and Miami are all plagued with senseless violent crime. Types of violent crime range from arson and burglary to assault, rape, and murder. The solution to this growing problem is not to build more and bigger prisons but rather to examine and deal with the causes: access to guns, drug use, and poverty.

Technique(s): _____

_____

4.   Misty, a five-month-old German shepherd puppy, goes to the hospital twice a week but not to see a veterinarian. At this Veteran's Administration hospital, Misty is helping doctors—not the other way around. In what may seem like a role reversal, animals like Misty are visiting the halls of human illness to relieve a type of pain doctors cannot treat. Their therapy is love, both giving it and helping others return it to them. Pets ranging from dogs to tropical fish are showing up as therapists in hospitals, nursing homes, and prisons.

Technique(s): _____

_____

5. One student looks at his neighbor's exam paper and quickly copies the answers. Another student finds out the questions on a test before her class takes it and tells her friends. Still another student sneaks a sheet of paper with formulas written on it into the test room. What about you? Would you be tempted to cheat on an exam if you knew you wouldn't get caught? According to a recent national survey, 40 percent of teenagers in the United States would cheat under that condition. What is causing this epidemic of cheating in schools? Most students cheat on tests because they feel pressure to get into a good college, because they want to avoid the hours of studying they need in order to get high grades, or simply because they are not concerned with honesty.

Technique(s): _____

_____

Thesis Statements

In the introduction, after you have presented some general background information, you need to narrow your focus. This is done in the *thesis statement*. A thesis statement is similar to a topic sentence. Just as a topic sentence controls the information for a paragraph, a thesis statement controls the information for an entire essay.

The thesis statement is a sentence that tells the reader what the essay will be about and what points you will make in the essay. Your thesis statement should state the subject of the essay, and list the main supporting points from your outline. The main supporting points should be listed in the order that you will present them in the essay.

WRITER'S TIP: Thesis Statements

The thesis statement:

- identifies the subject of the essay
- tells the focus of the subject by listing the main subtopics that the supporting paragraphs will develop
- may indicate the pattern of organization
- is usually the last sentence of the introduction.

Analyzing Thesis Statements

PRACTICE A **Underline the thesis statement in "Accidental Inventions" on pages 81–82 and answer the following questions.**

1. Does the thesis statement identify the subject of the essay? _____

2. Does it introduce examples of the subject that the essay develops? What are they?

_____

_____

_____

B Now look back at the sample introductions on pages 83 and 84 and underline the thesis statement in each one. Write the five thesis statements on the following lines.

1. _____

_____

2. _____

_____

3. _____

_____

4. _____

_____

5. _____

_____

C Look through several newspapers and magazines for interesting articles or find some on the Internet. Cut out or print out three examples of introductory paragraphs and bring them to class. In small groups, discuss what makes each paragraph effective or ineffective as an introduction. What techniques did the writers use?

The Body (Supporting Paragraphs)

The body of an essay is the longest part of the essay. It consists of several supporting paragraphs that support the thesis. Each supporting paragraph develops one point about the subject. Each paragraph begins with a topic sentence that is supported with specific details, facts, and examples.

> **WRITER'S TIP:** Supporting Paragraphs
>
> Each main idea that you wrote down in your outline will become one of the supporting paragraphs. For example, if you had three supporting ideas, you will have three supporting paragraphs.

Look again at the essay "Accidental Inventions" on pages 81–82.

1. Write the thesis statement here.

_____

_____

_____

2. What is the topic of the first supporting paragraph?

_____

3. What is the topic sentence of that paragraph? What is its main idea?

_____

_____

4. Does it develop the first point mentioned in the thesis statement? _____

5. What specific details are used for support?

_____

6. What is the topic of the second paragraph?

_____

_____

7. Does the topic sentence of that paragraph state its main idea? _____

8. What is the second point mentioned in the thesis statement?

_____

9. What specific details support it?

_____

10. What is the topic of the third supporting paragraph?

_____

_____

11. Does the topic sentence of that paragraph state its main idea? _____

12. What is the third point mentioned in the thesis statement?

_____

13. What specific details support it?

_____

The Conclusion

The final paragraph of your essay is the *conclusion*. It is the last thing your readers will see, so you want to make it interesting.

The purpose of this last paragraph is to summarize, without using the same words, the main points you have made in your essay. Your concluding paragraph should also leave your reader agreeing, disagreeing, or at least thinking about your thesis.

WRITER'S TIP: Conclusions

The purpose of the conclusion is to

- restate the thesis;

- summarize the main ideas; and

- leave your reader with something to think about.

There are no specific rules for writing a conclusion, but there are several techniques you can use. Many conclusions use one or a combination of the following techniques to wrap up the essay.

- **Restate your main points.**
  When you use this method of finishing your essay, you restate the main points you presented in your essay. Make sure that you do not repeat your exact words. Try to figure out a new way to say them.

- **Ask a question.**
  When you ask a provocative question, it will keep the readers thinking about the topic.

- **Suggest a solution; make a recommendation or prediction.**
  Depending on the topic of your essay, the conclusion might be a good place for you to suggest a solution to a problem that you have discussed, or to make a recommendation or a prediction.

It is often useful to use signal words or phrases in your conclusion.

TRANSITION SIGNALS THAT SIGNIFY A SUMMARY OR CONCLUSION

all in all	in conclusion	thus
consequently	in short	to conclude
finally	in summary	to summarize
in brief	therefore	

Note: These transition signals should be followed by a comma.

PRACTICE A **Read the conclusions. In small groups, identify the technique or techniques used in each one.**

1. In conclusion, although John Lennon is no longer with us, his music is still very much a part of people's lives. He was a remarkable individual who spoke in a language that everyone could relate to. During the turbulent 1960s and 1970s, his optimistic message of peace, love, and happiness emerged. Today, perhaps more than ever, people recall the themes of his songs and look to them for answers. In the years to come, I predict that Lennon's message will continue to inspire countless generations.

   Technique(s): _____

   _____

2. Thus, although sleep research is a relatively new field, it is a topic arousing considerable interest. A decade ago, only a handful of sleep disorder centers existed; however, today there are more than seventy-five. Consequently, scientists are beginning to unlock the mysteries of what Shakespeare called the "chief nourisher in life's feast." Still, there are numerous chapters to be added to the bedtime story. And then problem sleepers will be able to rest easy.

Technique(s): _____

_____

3. During his life, Peter gained a great deal of power and influenced the course of Russian history. In summary, although he was not always completely successful, he worked very hard to modernize and westernize Russia. Although his actions were not always popular, everything Peter did was in the best interest of his country. By the end of his life, Peter had made significant progress toward achieving his goal of transforming Russia. Therefore, in my opinion, he deserves the name Peter the Great.

Technique(s): _____

_____

4. Car manufactures continue to make technological improvements on their vehicles, and it is no coincidence that today's generation of cars is the safest ever. Crash tests demonstrate that many of today's cars earn top ratings for safety. However, real-life use will always demonstrate what we already know: that cars are only as safe as the people driving them.

Technique(s): _____

_____

5. When Michael Jordan retired from the game that made him the richest, most famous sportsman in the world, basketball lost one of its brightest stars. Jordan retired for the third and final time on April 16, 2003, leaving a sporting legacy many people believed would remain permanently unmatched. We will always remember him for his talent, his competitive personality, and his unbelievable ability to stay in the air when all the other players were already going down. Will there ever be another sports icon as great as Michael Jordan?

Technique(s): _____

_____

_____

_____

6. As I have shown, low-income senior citizens make up approximately 30 percent of the elderly population. These people are among the most vulnerable members of society because they depend so heavily on government programs for food, shelter, and medical needs. They are the ones who will suffer most severely if the government cuts back on its social programs.

Technique(s): _____

_____

 B Look through several newspapers and magazines for interesting articles or find some on the Internet. Cut out or print out three examples of concluding paragraphs and bring them to class. In small groups, discuss what makes each paragraph effective or ineffective as a conclusion. What techniques did the writers use?

The Title

All essays have a title. A good title for an essay has two functions:

- to suggest the subject of the essay
- to spark the reader's interest

Although it is not always necessary to write a title for a paragraph, it is important to write a title for an essay. Follow the same rules for writing a title of an essay as you did for writing the title of a paragraph. While the title is the first part of your essay your reader sees, it is usually easier to come up with a good title after you have written your essay.

USING THE WRITING PROCESS TO WRITE AN ESSAY

You are going to write a five-paragraph essay about the pressures of being a student. You may determine your purpose and audience.

 ### Step 1: Prewriting

Remember that the hardest part of writing is often *getting started.* To generate some ideas, try *brainstorming, clustering, freewriting,* or *keeping a journal* about the subject: the pressures of being a student. Then look over what you have written and decide on a focus for your essay. For example, are you going to discuss the pressures of being a student in a foreign country or in your native country? Are you going to talk about the pressures of being a high school student, college student, and/or graduate student? Are you going to talk about financial, academic, social, and/or emotional pressures?

After you decide on a focus, you can write a thesis statement that expresses your focus. You can always modify your thesis statement after you make your outline.

Sometimes it is difficult to decide on the supporting points to use in your essay. Even after you have done some prewriting, you may still need to do more thinking and planning to find a focus.

The next exercise will help you learn how to find a focus for an essay. Then you can apply what you learned to find a focus for the essay you are writing on the pressures of being a student.

Finding a Focus

There are a number of common ways to divide a general subject into three parts that you can use for the supporting paragraphs. For example, if your general subject is *the effects of the Internet,* there are several possible ways you could divide it. You might think about *time* and describe the effects of the Internet in the past, present, and future. Or you might consider *people* and write about the effects on children, adults, and the elderly. Still another way would be to analyze the effects of the Internet on society by writing about the economic, educational, and social effects.

The following chart provides additional suggestions for how to divide a broad subject:

PLACE	PEOPLE
a. local **b.** national **c.** international	**a.** students **b.** workers **c.** retired people
a. home **b.** work **c.** school	**a.** family **b.** friends **c.** coworkers
a. land **b.** sea **c.** air	**a.** children **b.** adults **c.** the elderly
TIME	SOCIETY
a. past **b.** present **c.** future	**a.** economic **b.** political **c.** social/educational/religious
a. childhood **b.** adulthood **c.** old age	**a.** business **b.** science **c.** the arts

PRACTICE **A** **Practice finding a focus for each of these essay prompts. Work with a partner. Think of three main points that you could use to develop an essay. You may use ideas from the preceding chart or come up with ideas of your own.**

1. Why do you like (or dislike) your present job? (*Hint:* Give three reasons.)

   Main points: a. <u>flexible hours</u>

                b. <u>good pay</u>

                c. <u>friendly co-workers</u>

2. What are the benefits of learning English? (*Hint:* Give benefits of learning English that involve three areas of your life.)

   Main points: a. _____

                b. _____

                c. _____

3. What skill do you think a person needs to be successful in the modern world? (*Hint:* Give three reasons to support your choice.)

Main points: a. _____

b. _____

c. _____

4. What are some ways to reduce stress in your life? (*Hint:* Give examples of three ways to reduce stress.)

Main points: a. _____

b. _____

c. _____

5. Who do you think has made the greatest change in our world in the past 100 years? (*Hint:* Give three reasons to support your choice.)

Main points: a. _____

b. _____

c. _____

6. Describe a custom from your country that you think people from other countries should adopt. (*Hint:* Give three reasons to support your choice.)

Main points: a. _____

b. _____

c. _____

B **Make a plan for your essay. Write a simple outline of the ideas you generated from prewriting about the pressures of being a student to help you organize your thoughts as you plan your essay. Use your outline as a guide and refer to it while you are writing.**

Topic: The pressures of being a _____ (high school, college, foreign, graduate, other kind of) student

Main points: 1. _____

_____

2. _____

_____

3. _____

_____

Step 2: Writing

After you have spent some time prewriting, you are ready for the next step in the writing process: writing the first draft of your essay. Begin with the introduction.

(A) **Write an introduction. On a separate piece of paper, write the introduction for a five-paragraph essay on *the pressures of being a student*. Follow these steps:**

1. Decide what technique(s) you want to use to introduce your subject. Would an anecdote be effective? What about a quotation or some facts?

2. Write a thesis statement.

3. Work with a partner. Read and discuss each other's introductions.

(B) **Write topic sentences. Look at your outline. Write a topic sentence for each supporting paragraph on the following lines.**

Topic sentence for first supporting paragraph: _____

_____

Topic sentence for second supporting paragraph: _____

_____

Topic sentence for third supporting paragraph: _____

_____

(C) **Write the first draft. On a separate piece of paper, write a first draft of the supporting paragraphs for your essay on *the pressures of being a student*. Follow the principles you learned in Chapter 2 for writing effective paragraphs. Use the topic sentences you just wrote for each of the three paragraphs and support them with details, facts, or examples.**

Ordering Supporting Paragraphs to Create a Coherent Essay

The way you arrange your paragraphs depends on the kind of essay you are writing. For example, if you are describing a process, the logical organization of paragraphs will be chronological—that is, arranged according to *time order*. If you are writing an essay describing what your favorite place to relax looks like, you will use *spatial order* to organize the paragraphs according to where things are located. On the other hand, if you are discussing examples, causes, effects, or reasons, you will probably use *order of importance*. With this type of organization, you might begin with the least important item and end with the most important one.

PRACTICE (A) **Read the following paragraphs. Number them in the correct order so they form a coherent five-paragraph essay.**

_____ First of all, one of my favorite competition reality shows is *Top Chef*. *Top Chef* revolves around a group of aspiring chefs who compete in a variety of cooking challenges to win a prize of $200,000 to start their own restaurant and a feature article in *Food and Wine* magazine. Each week, the contestants compete in two challenges. In the first challenge, contestants have a short time to show their basic cooking abilities. During the second challenge, the chefs take part in a longer, more difficult task where they must show their creativity and originality. Contestants cook three-course meals for a group of hungry diners and a panel of judges. The contestants are often asked to prepare gourmet meals with unusual ingredients such as American junk food or exotic seafood like eel. Each week, one of the aspiring chefs is asked to leave until the end of the season when the proud winner is chosen.

_____ *Project Runway* is another popular competition reality show that I enjoy watching. This show centers on fashion instead of food. Each week, aspiring fashion designers compete to create the best clothes using certain materials. A panel of famous fashion designers judge the clothes, and one or more contestants are eliminated each week. The final winner receives a $150,000 prize to start his or her own line of clothes. In some of the most memorable episodes, contestants have been asked to design clothes using anything from garden plants and flowers to recyclable trash such as rubber tires and plastic bottles. Whatever the challenge, these aspiring fashion designers never fail to create clothes that could one day be found at a store near you!

_____ Recently there has been an explosion in a type of television programming called reality TV. As the name suggests, reality TV is about real people in real situations. Unlike traditional television shows, reality TV shows are unscripted, so viewers can watch how real people react in certain situations. There are many types of reality shows, but my favorite shows are competition reality programs. In these programs average people with special skills compete against one another over an entire season. Each week, competitions are held in which participants exhibit a particular skill. At the end of every episode, one person is eliminated from the program until, at the end of the season, only one contestant remains. The winner receives a prize, which is usually a large sum of money and some sort of professional contract. Three of my favorite competition reality shows are *Top Chef, Project Runway,* and *American Idol,* which showcase talents including cooking, fashion design, and singing.

_____ As you can see, competition reality shows are my favorite in the reality television genre. Some people say that it's the interesting contestants that keep them watching. Others believe the critique of the judges is the key to success. However, one thing is certainly true: whether it's a new recipe you're craving, the scoop on the latest trends in fashion, or just a good old-fashioned song, competition-based reality programs have something for everyone.

_____ Finally, while *Top Chef* and *Project Runway* are always exciting to watch, my personal favorite competition reality show is *American Idol.* Each season begins with auditions held around the country. After weeks of auditions, a panel of famous judges picks the top performers to go to Hollywood, California. There, judges narrow down a group of a hundred talented singers to just twelve finalists. These singers go on to compete on live TV. Unlike *Top Chef* and *Project Runway,* where a group of judges controls the outcome of the show, people watching the show choose the winner of *American Idol.* Each week, the finalists perform a song in front of a live audience, and the judges watch and critique each finalist. As soon as the show ends, viewers phone in, text, or go online to vote for their favorite performer. The next day, the host of the show tells which singer received the fewest votes from viewers, and that person is sent home. The process continues until one person remains. Finally, after twelve weeks, he or she is crowned the *American Idol* and wins a $350,000 recording contract with a major music label. So far, winners of *American Idol* have become some of the most successful pop stars in the United States, including country singer Carrie Underwood and pop singer Kelly Clarkson.

B **Work with a partner. Compare the way you numbered the paragraphs.**

Linking Supporting Paragraphs

You have learned that the sentences within a paragraph should flow smoothly. Similarly, the paragraphs within an essay should flow smoothly. Each supporting paragraph needs to be clearly linked to the one that came before it. There are several ways to guide your reader from one paragraph to the next. Good writers connect the first sentence of each new supporting paragraph to the thesis statement or to the previous paragraph.

There are three common ways to connect paragraphs in an essay:

1. Repeat key words or ideas from the thesis statement.

2. Refer to words or ideas from the preceding paragraph.

3. Use transitional expressions.

Refer back to the essay "Accidental Inventions" on page 81. Notice how the topic sentences for each body paragraph connects back to the thesis or the previous paragraph.

Thesis statement from "Accidental Inventions": *Three of the most well-known inventions or discoveries that happened by accident are popsicles, microwave ovens, and penicillin.*

Each supporting paragraph in the essay is connected to the thesis or to the previous paragraph.

Topic sentence for first body paragraph: *Popsicles were invented by accident by an eleven-year-old boy named Frank Epperson.*

Explanation: In this topic sentence, the writer uses the words "invented by accident" to refer back to the thesis statement.

Topic sentence for second body paragraph: *Like popsicles, microwave ovens were an accidental discovery.*

Explanation: In this topic sentence, the writer links the paragraph to the one before it by referring to "popsicles." The writer also connects it to the thesis with the words "an accidental discovery."

Topic sentence for third body paragraph: *Finally, while popsicles are good to eat and microwave ovens make cooking faster and easier, one accidental discovery, penicillin, has saved millions of lives since its discovery in 1928.*

Explanation: In this topic sentence, the writer begins a transition, "Finally," as a linking method. The writer also links this paragraph to the previous paragraphs by referring to popsicles and microwave ovens. Finally, the writer uses the key words "one accidental discovery" to connect this paragraph to the thesis statement.

WRITER'S TIP: Listing Transitions

It is often helpful to use listing transitions such as *first of all, second, another, also, in addition, finally,* and the like in the topic sentences supporting your essay.

Write a conclusion. Reread the introduction and supporting paragraphs you wrote on "The Pressures of Being a Student." On a separate piece of paper, write the conclusion to this essay.

Putting Together the First Draft

On a separate piece of paper, put together your introduction, three supporting paragraphs, and conclusion. This will be the first draft of your entire essay. Add a title that gives readers a good idea of what the essay is about. Save your paper. Your next step will be to revise it.

 ## Step 3: Revise and Edit Your Essay

Remember, writing is a process that involves revising and editing. After you have written the first draft of your essay, you need to revise and edit it. The first thing you need to do is reread the whole essay. Keep in mind that your essay is a group of related paragraphs about one main idea.

> **WRITER'S TIP:** Take a Break
>
> Take a break from your writing. It is helpful to put your draft away for at least a day before you begin to revise it.

As you revise and edit, try to improve your first draft.

1. Your essay should have an introduction that gets the reader's attention and states the main idea in a thesis statement. It should also have several supporting paragraphs, each with a topic sentence that supports one aspect of the main idea of the essay. Finally, it should include a conclusion that ties the whole essay together. As you read the draft, make sure that you have included all three parts of an essay.

2. You also need to make sure that your essay is well organized. Ask yourself if the ideas follow a logical sequence from paragraph to paragraph. If the order is confusing, move the paragraphs around so that your main points are organized logically—for example, in time order, spatial order, or order of importance.

3. In addition, you need to pay attention to individual sentences within paragraphs. Remember that each paragraph must develop one main supporting point stated in the topic sentence. If a sentence in a paragraph does not support the main idea of the paragraph, you should delete it, rewrite it, or move it to another paragraph in the essay.

4. Make sure you have not left out any important points or relevant information that would help support your topic or prove your thesis. If so, you need to add a sentence or paragraph to improve your essay.

5. Finally, edit your essay by checking the grammar, punctuation, and spelling. Correct any mistakes you find.

A Reread the draft of the essay you wrote on the pressures of being a student. Answer the questions.

1. What is the subject of your essay?

   _____

2. What is the purpose of your essay?

   _____

3. Who is your audience?

   _____

B Revise your essay by answering each of the following questions.

REVISING CHECKLIST FOR ESSAYS	YES	NOT YET
1. Does the title of the essay give readers a good idea of what the essay is about?		
2. Does the introduction create interest in the topic for readers?		
3. Does the introduction state the main idea and the focus of the essay in a clear thesis statement?		
4. Does the first (second, third) supporting paragraph have a topic sentence that clearly states the first (second, third) main supporting point?		
5. Does every sentence in that paragraph support the topic sentence?		
6. Have irrelevant sentences been eliminated so that the paragraph has unity?		
7. Are the sentences in the paragraph arranged in a logical order?		
8. Are there transitions in the paragraph to guide the reader from one idea to the next?		
9. Do the supporting paragraphs provide adequate support and enough specific information to develop and prove the thesis of the essay?		
10. Are the supporting paragraphs arranged in a logical order?		
11. Does the conclusion summarize the main ideas of the essay?		

If the answer to any of the questions is "not yet," go back and try to improve your essay.

C *Peer Revising.* Sometimes it is helpful to have someone else read your paper and offer suggestions on ways to improve it. Exchange drafts with a classmate and read each other's essay. Use the worksheet below as a guide for suggesting improvements in your partner's essay.

PEER REVISION WORKSHEET

Writer: _____   Peer Editor: _____

1. What are the strengths of the essay? _____

   _____

   _____

2. What did you like best about it? _____

   _____

   _____

3. What weaknesses did you notice? _____

   _____

   _____

4. What suggestions for improvement can you offer? _____

   _____

   _____

5. Is there any information that doesn't belong in the paper? If so, what would you suggest deleting?

   _____

   _____

6. Does anything seem to be missing from this paper? If so, what would you suggest adding?

   _____

   _____

D Incorporate any suggestions your partner has made that you agree with.

E Use the checklist on page 75 to edit your essay. Correct all the grammar, punctuation, capitalization, and spelling errors before you rewrite it.

ON YOUR OWN

A Discuss the questions in the chart with a partner and record your answers. Then, choose one question to write about. Write a five-paragraph essay that explains your preference. Use specific reasons to develop your essay. Don't forget to include an introduction, several body paragraphs, and a conclusion.

WHICH DO YOU PREFER?	YOU	YOUR PARTNER
a. Living in a big city **b.** Living in a small town		
a. Going to a school where you are required to wear a uniform **b.** Going to a school where you can wear anything you want		
a. Eating out at restaurants **b.** Cooking at home		
a. Attending a big university **b.** Attending a small college		
a. Spending your money as you earn it **b.** Saving your money for the future		
a. Attending a live performance (or sporting event) **b.** Watching the same event on television		
a. Traveling with a companion **b.** Traveling alone		
a. Face-to-face communication **b.** Other types of communication, such as email, phone calls, texting, social media		
a. Taking public transportation **b.** Driving yourself		

B Choose one of the other topics on pages 91–92 and write a five-paragraph essay.

CHAPTER HIGHLIGHTS

Discuss the following questions with a partner.

1. What are the three main parts of an essay? What is the purpose of each part?

2. What are some techniques you can use to write an introduction?

3. What are some techniques you can use to write a conclusion?

PART 2

TYPES OF ESSAYS

Now that you have learned the basic structure of an essay, you will practice writing several different types of essays. There are many kinds of essays. Sometimes your teacher will decide which type of essay you should write. But other times it may be up to you to choose a type of essay that fits your purpose.

Here are some of the common types of essays and their purposes:

ESSAY TYPE	PURPOSE
Process	To describe a sequence of steps that explain how to do something or how something works
Division and Classification	To describe logical divisions of a topic and organize or sort things into categories
Causes and Effects	To analyze why things happen (the causes) or explain what happened as a result of something (the effects)
Comparison and Contrast	To show the similarities or differences between two things
Problem-Solution	To describe a problem and evaluate possible solutions

The chapters in Part 2 will give you practice writing some of the common types of essays. In this way, you will learn how using these patterns can help you organize your ideas.

When your purpose in writing is to inform your readers about how to do something or to describe the order of steps in a procedure, you will write a *process essay*. For instance, when you explain procedures such as how to program a cell phone, how to give a good haircut, or how to study for a math test, you are describing steps in a process.

WRITER'S TIP: Time Order

When you organize the steps in a process, you should arrange them according to the order in which the steps occur. This is called time order or chronological order.

EXPLAINING STEPS IN A PROCESS

In academic writing, process essays are often used in the scientific and technical fields. For example, they are used to describe biological processes such as how food is digested, chemical processes such as photosynthesis, and technical processes such as how a diesel engine works. Process essays can also have practical applications, such as explaining how to choose a major or how to find a new job.

Copyright 2005 by Randy Glasbergen.
www.glasbergen.com

"I need you to write a manual to interpret the brochure
that we created to clarify the pamphlet that we printed
to define the handout that we sent to explain the memo."

The Language of Process: Useful Phrases and Sentence Patterns

Process essays are organized according to time. When you write a process essay, you should begin by describing the first step in the process and continue in time until you have described the last step in the process. Transition words help the reader understand the sequence of the steps. Here are some common transition words used in process essays.

TRANSITION WORDS FOR A PROCESS ESSAY		
first	soon afterward	every time
the first step	the third step	whenever
from then on	then	meanwhile
next	at this point	while
the next step	as	during
before	as soon as	the last step
after	when	finally
after that		

PRACTICE **Complete the paragraph with words and phrases from the chart.**

Do you avoid parking on busy streets because you are not good at parallel parking? Believe it or not, parallel parking is not as difficult as you think, especially if you follow these steps. _____, find a parking spot that is big enough for your car. _____, use your turn signal to let other drivers know that you are going to park. _____, pull ahead of the spot until you are next to the car parked in front of the spot. Your rear bumper should be even with that car's rear bumper. _____, put the car in reverse and start backing up slowly. _____ the car starts moving, turn the wheel as far as it will go toward the curb and back slowly and carefully into the space. _____ your front door is even with the rear bumper of the car in front of you, begin turning the steering wheel in the opposite direction—away from the curb. Continue to turn the steering wheel away from the curb as you slowly back into the space. _____, straighten out the steering wheel and drive forward or back in the space until your car is centered between the car in front of you and the one behind you.

THESIS STATEMENTS FOR PROCESS ESSAYS

The following sentence patterns are useful in writing thesis statements for process essays:

1. It is { easy / simple / not difficult } to _____ if you have the right { tools. / equipment. / materials. / ingredients. }

   *It is easy **to** change a flat tire **if you have the right** equipment.*

   *It is easy **to** build a platform bed **if you have the right** materials.*

   *It is not difficult **to** make a cheese soufflé **if you have the right** ingredients.*

2. _____ is easy when you follow { these steps. / these directions. / these instructions. / this procedure. }

   *Making a delicious omelet **is easy when you follow** these steps.*

   *Impressing your boss **is easy when you follow** these instructions.*

   *Parallel parking **is easy when you follow** these directions.*

3. There are { three / four / several } major steps involved in _____.

   *There are three **major steps involved in** studying for an exam.*

   *There are several **major steps involved in** growing a vegetable garden.*

   *There are several **major steps involved in** writing a good paragraph.*

PRACTICE **Write a thesis statement for a process essay on each of these essay topics. Use a variety of sentence patterns.**

1. **Topic:** How to write an essay

   Thesis statement: <u>Writing a good essay is easier if you follow three main steps.</u>

2. **Topic:** How to impress your teacher or boss

   Thesis statement: _____

   _____

3. **Topic:** How to stay in shape

   Thesis statement: _____

   _____

4. **Topic:** How to make a pizza

   Thesis statement: _____

   _____

5. **Topic:** How to build a tree house

   Thesis statement: _____

   _____

6. **Topic:** The best way to lose weight

   Thesis statement: _____

   _____

7. **Topic:** How to make a beautiful flower arrangement

   Thesis statement: _____

   _____

8. **Topic:** How to decorate your dorm room

   Thesis statement: _____

   _____

9. **Topic:** How to pack for a weekend trip

   Thesis statement: _____

   _____

10. **Topic:** How to quit smoking

    Thesis statement: _____

    _____

11. **Topic:** How to network for a new job

Thesis statement: _____

_____

12. **Topic:** How to relax after a stressful day at work or school

Thesis statement: _____

_____

13. **Topic:** How to make new friends

Thesis statement: _____

_____

WRITING PROCESS PARAGRAPHS

Paragraph 1

A **You have just made a bookcase in a woodworking class. Now you need to write a one-paragraph description of the process for your teacher. Look at the ten step-by-step drawings.**

1. Assemble wood, nails, glue, a hammer, a saw, sandpaper, and paint.

2. Cut 2 side pieces—11″ by 28″; 3 pieces for top, bottom, and shelf—11″ by 13½″; 1 back piece—15″ by 28″; and two 10″ molding strips.

3. Sand each piece of wood.

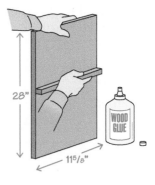

4. Glue one molding strip to each side piece, 14″ down from top.

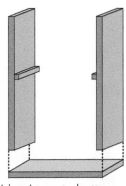

5. Nail the side pieces to bottom.

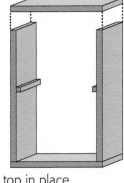

6. Nail the top in place.

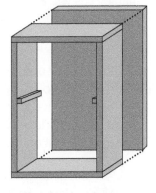

7. Nail the back piece in place.

8. Paint the bookcase and shelf.

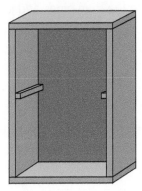

9. Let dry 2 hours.

10. Slide the shelf into place.

B On a separate piece of paper, write a one-paragraph description of the process. Use the drawings as a guide. Be sure to include a topic sentence that states your purpose and transition signals to indicate the order of the steps. Add a title.

Paragraph 2

A Read the following conversation between a student and a librarian.

Student: Excuse me. I'm doing research for a paper I'm writing about the effects of global warming on marine life. Can you tell me how to find some current articles on this subject?

Librarian: Certainly. The best place to begin is over here in the reference section. Are you familiar with how to use a computerized periodic index?

Student: Not really. I've only used it once, and I think I've forgotten how it works.

Librarian: It's really quite easy. All you need to do is type in your topic here and press the return key. The computer will search its database of newspapers, magazines, and journals and will give you a list of all the articles related to your topic. You can choose which ones you want to look up, and you can print out the list of citations.

Student: OK. That seems fairly easy. But my professor said we could only use articles from the past three years.

Librarian: That's no problem. The dates of the articles are given right here, so you can just look up the most recent ones.

Student: That's great. Is there anything else I need to know?

Librarian: Well, another good feature of this program is that it gives you a brief summary of the main points of the article.

Student: How can I look at that?

Librarian: Just click on the box that says *abstract*. Here, I'll show you. Also, if the article is available in electronic form, there will be a link labeled "Electronic access." Click on this link. It will take you to the opening screen for the magazine, newspaper, or journal; and you can choose the issue you want from there. If the article is available in print form, write down the call number. Then, you're ready to find it on the shelf.

Student: Thank you so much for helping me.

Librarian: You're welcome. If you have any more questions, I'll be at the reference desk.

Student: Oh, one more thing before you go. Where are the magazines and journals?

Librarian: They're in the periodical section on the second floor. You can't take them out, but there are several copy machines in that area if you need to make a copy of any of the articles.

Student: Thanks again.

B **Using information from the conversation, write a paragraph about how to use a computerized index to do research.**

_____

_____

_____

_____

_____

_____

_____

_____

_____

ANALYZING A PROCESS ESSAY

 Read the process essay below that a student wrote.

How to Make an Object Disappear

Have you ever wondered how magicians perform their amazing tricks? I am not a professional magician, but I do magic tricks as a hobby. For example, I can bend a strong metal spoon with my bare hands, make a deck of cards leap out of my lap, or even shrink a pen to half its original size! Most people love to watch magic tricks because it is a challenge to figure out how it's done. However, traditionally, magicians are never supposed to reveal the secrets behind their illusions. In fact, if any of my magician friends knew what I was about to tell you they would probably never speak to me again. However, I feel that everyone should learn how to do at least one magic trick. It doesn't take a genius to learn most of the tricks I perform; but if you follow these steps, you'll look like one to the people you trick.

The first thing you need to do is decide what type of trick you want to perform. Some of my favorite tricks involve making something disappear. People are always amazed when something that is right in front of them suddenly vanishes. So let's say you decide to learn a trick that makes an object disappear into thin air. You'll need to decide what object to use. For your first trick, I suggest using a coin, such as a quarter, as the object of the illusion.

At this point you need to learn and memorize the basic steps of the trick. First, sit down at a table opposite a spectator and place a quarter on the table. Then, slide your left hand back towards you as if you are picking up the quarter, but instead of picking up the coin, you knock it into your lap. Quickly, make a fist and pretend the quarter is in there. Next, pretend to pass the coin to your right hand in order to confuse your audience. Say some magic words and then open your hand—and the coin is magically gone! If the viewer says that it is in your other hand, open it to show that the quarter has disappeared into thin air.

The next, and most important step in perfecting a new trick is practice, practice, practice! Find a table in your house and a mirror so you can watch yourself and spot any mistakes you might make. You can also video yourself and watch the video to see what parts of the trick you need to improve. You need to learn the trick so well that you do not have to look down at your hands while you are performing it. This way you will look confident and can make eye contact with your audience, which is an important part of the performance. If you look at your hands, it is likely that your audience will, too. Finally, you need to practice what you are going to say while you are performing the trick. A patter, which is the term magicians use for what they say while doing a magic trick, is a big part of pulling off any trick. This is a great way to distract your audience.

As you can see, it is not very difficult to learn a magic trick. Of course, like any other performance art, magic requires a lot of practice and personality. Remember to keep your audience engaged by talking to them and looking at them the whole time you are performing the trick. Don't be shy about trying out your tricks with relatives or friends or even a stranger. Everyone will be impressed with your showmanship and fooled by your quick moves. Magic is a wonderful way to engage the people around you and keep your mind active by learning new ways to fool your audience.

B **Work with a partner. Answer the following questions.**

1. What technique does the student use to introduce the topic? (See Chapter 4.)

   _____

2. What process is the student describing?

   _____

3. How is the information organized?

   _____

4. Make a list of the main steps in the process.

   a. _____

   b. _____

   c. _____

5. What transitions did the student use to connect the ideas in the essay? Underline them.

6. What audience do you think the student had in mind when he wrote this essay?

   _____

ESSAY PLAN: Process

Use the following plan as a guide when you write a process essay.

PROCESS ESSAY PLAN

Introduction
1. State what the process is and why it is important.
2. Define the process.
3. State the purpose for explaining the process.
4. List any equipment, ingredients, or supplies needed to perform the process.
5. Write a thesis statement that states the topic and explains that a series of steps is required.

Supporting Paragraphs
1. Include a topic sentence for each supporting paragraph that states the main step and its purpose.
2. Describe the steps in the process, using time order.
3. If there are a lot of steps, group them into several main stages.

Conclusion
1. Review why the process is important.
2. Summarize the main steps in the process without the details.

WRITER'S TIP: Audience

Keep your audience in mind while you are writing a process essay. Ask yourself, "What do my readers know about my topic?" This will help you decide what steps and terms need more or less explanation.

WRITING A PROCESS ESSAY

In this activity, you will practice writing an essay that describes the steps in a process.

 Prewriting

A **Choose one of the following topics or your own topic to write about. Make a list of steps in the process on the lines that follow.**

How to . . .

• wash a car

• make rice, tea, a salad, noodles, etc.

• write a good paragraph or essay

• study for an exam

• annoy your teacher, your boss, or your parents

• make a paper airplane, knit a scarf, paint a picture, etc.

_____

_____

_____

_____

_____

_____

_____

_____

_____

_____

B **Organize the steps according to time order. Prepare an informal outline.**

TOPIC: How to _____

 Writing

On a separate piece of paper, write the first draft of your essay. Use the essay plan on page 111 to help you draft your essay. Be sure to provide some background information about the process in the introduction and include a clear thesis sentence that states your purpose. Describe the steps in the supporting paragraphs and organize them according to time order. End with a conclusion that summarizes the steps and restates the purpose.

 Revising and Editing

A *Personal Revising.* **Wait at least one day and then revise your essay using the checklist on page 97. Also, make sure that you have adequately described each step in the process. Write or type a revised version of your essay.**

B *Peer Revising.* **Exchange drafts with a classmate. Use the following worksheet as a guide for suggesting improvements in your partner's essay.**

PEER REVISION WORKSHEET

Writer: _____ Peer Editor: _____

1. What are the strengths of the essay? _____

   _____

   _____

2. Does the introduction identify the process and state why it is important? _____ yes _____ no

3. What weaknesses, if any, are there in the organization? _____

   _____

   _____

4. What suggestions can you offer to improve the organization? _____

   _____

   _____

5. Are there enough transitions to guide you from one step to the next? _____ yes _____ no

6. Is each step in the process adequately explained? _____ yes _____ no

7. Is the conclusion effective? _____ yes _____ no

   If not, how can it be improved? _____

   _____

   _____

C **Incorporate any suggestions your partner has made that you agree with.**

D *Editing.* **Use the checklist on page 75 to edit your essay. Correct all the grammar, punctuation, capitalization, and spelling errors before you rewrite it.**

GO ONLINE

Use the Internet to find instructions for how to do or make something that interests you. Some of the most popular sites are http://www.ehow.com, http://www.wikihow.com and http://www.instructables.com.

Here are some suggestions:

- juggle three balls
- create a website
- plant a garden
- bake bread
- refinish a table
- make an origami crane

Then use the information to write a process essay.

YOU BE THE EDITOR

The following recipe has seven mistakes. Correct the mistakes on the recipe card.

If you like to eat or bake delicious cookies, you will love this recipe.

Soften ½ pound of butter and mix it with 2 cups off sugar. Stir in 3 beaten egg and 3 tablespoons of lemon juice. Then add 4 cups of flour 1 teaspoon of baking powder, and 2 ½ teaspoons of nutmeg. As soon as the mixture is thoroughly combined, form the dough into a large ball and refrigerator it for at least 1 hour. When your ready to bake the cookies, divide the ball of dough in half. Roll the dough out so that is ½ inch thick. It will be easier if you use a rolling pin. Cut the cookies into shapes, using the open end of a glass or cookie cutters if you have them. Put the cookies on greased cookie sheets and bake them at 375° for 6 minutes. To make them sweeter and more appetizing, frost them with colored frosting and add sprinkles. Don't eat to many!

ON YOUR OWN

Choose a topic and write a process essay. Here are some suggested topics:

- How to find a job
- How to apply to a university in your country or the United States
- How to make up with a friend after an argument
- How to start a business
- How to do a search on the Internet
- How to impress your boss
- How to do a Sudoku puzzle
- How to organize your closet

CHAPTER 6 Division and Classification Essays

....
LEARNING OUTCOME **Essay Writing:** Use the writing process to write a division and classification essay
....

Division and classification is another way to organize information for an essay. A broad or complex topic is often easier to write about when you divide it into parts and then classify the parts into groups that have something in common. In other words, you divide a topic into groups of items that share similar characteristics.

Division and classification essays are useful in academic writing. For example, in a business class, you might be asked to classify and discuss the types of insurance policies. In a civics class, you might need to describe the three branches of the U.S. government. In a chemistry class, you might have to group types of chemical reactions.

GLASBERGEN
© Randy Glasbergen
glasbergen.com

"The 4 basic food groups are things my doctor won't let me eat, things my wife won't let me eat, things my heartburn won't let me eat and things my teeth won't let me eat."

WRITER'S TIP: Grouping Ideas

It is helpful to find at least three separate divisions or groups to use. For example, if you were writing an essay about the types of government in the United States, you could classify them into three groups according to where each one has authority: federal, state, and local. Make sure the groups do not overlap.

The prewriting (including planning) stage is a very important part of the process of writing a classification essay. Before you write, you need to spend time thinking about your topic and how you want to divide it into groups.

Clustering is a good technique to use to help you identify groups. Look at the two examples of clustering.

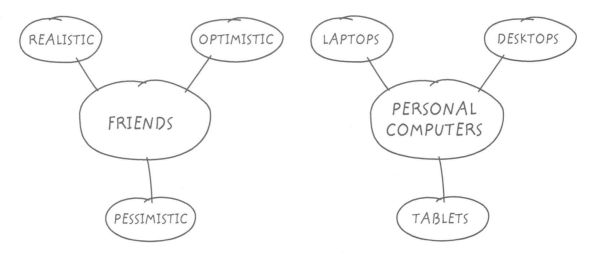

DIVIDING A TOPIC INTO GROUPS

To write a division-classification essay, you should begin by deciding **how** you will divide your topic into groups (or types, categories, kinds, etc.). That means choosing a basis of division or classification. Then, divide your topic into several complete and separate groups. Each paragraph in the body of the essay explains or describes one of the groups. The number of groups will equal the number of supporting paragraphs in your essay.

In the first example, if you want to write an essay about your friends, you can choose their outlooks on life as a basis of division. Then you can divide your friends into three groups: optimistic, pessimistic, and realistic. Your essay will have three supporting paragraphs. You will describe optimistic people in one supporting paragraph, pessimistic people in another supporting paragraph, and realistic people in the third supporting paragraph. Remember to give examples of the characteristics of people in each group, so that the reader can see how each group is distinct from the others.

In the second example, you could divide the topic of types of personal computers into three groups according to their size: laptops, desktops, and tablets. You would describe desktop computers in one supporting paragraph, laptop computers in another supporting paragraph, and tablets in the third supporting paragraph. Provide examples of the characteristics of each type so the reader can see how each group is unique.

Dividing a Topic

There is often more than one way to divide a topic into groups. The important thing to remember is that you must choose one basis for dividing the topic. For example, the subject *cars* can be classified into groups by size: compact, intermediate, and full size. Cars can also be classified in other ways such as by manufacturer, price, body style, or fuel efficiency.

The way you divide your topic depends on the purpose of your essay. The groups you choose must be separate and distinct. In other words, the groups must not overlap. For example, if you were writing an essay on types of clothes, you might use the following groups: formal clothes, work clothes, and casual clothes. In this case, the basis for division would be where the clothes are worn. You could also classify clothes according to season and have four groups: spring clothes, summer clothes, fall clothes, and winter clothes. But you could not divide clothes into casual clothes, work clothes, and summer clothes because the groups overlap. A pair of shorts could be put into the casual clothes group and into the summer clothes group. Similarly, a linen suit fits in two of the groups: work clothes and summer clothes.

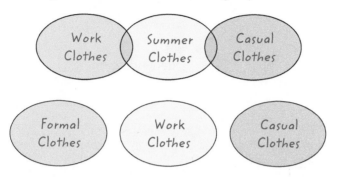

PRACTICE A **How many ways can you think of to divide the students in your class into groups? Work with a partner and make a list of several different ways. Identify the basis of division for each one and list the groups.**

1. **Basis for Division:** _Dominant hand_

   Groups:

   right-handed

   left-handed

2. **Basis for Division:** _____

   Groups:

   _____

   _____

3. **Basis for Division:** _____

   Groups:

   _____

   _____

4. **Basis for Division:** _____

   Groups:

   _____

   _____

B **Have a class discussion. Talk about the ways you divided your classmates.**

THE LANGUAGE OF CLASSIFICATION:
Useful Sentence Patterns for Thesis Statements

The following sentence patterns are useful in writing topic sentences and thesis statements for division-classification paragraphs and essays:

1. There are { two / three / four / several } { kinds / types / classes } of _____ depending on _____: _____

Examples:

There are three types *of elementary schools in our city* **depending on** *how they are funded: public, private, and charter.*

There are three kinds *of burns* **depending on** *how deep each one penetrates the skin's surface: first degree, second degree, or third degree.*

2. I can { divide / classify / group / categorize } _____ into three { parts / groups / types / kinds } according to _____: _____.

Examples:

I can classify *my friends* **into three** *groups* **according to** *where I met them: school friends, work friends, and neighborhood friends.*

I can divide *my professors* **into three** *groups* **according to** *how available they are to students: rarely available, available only for office hours, and almost always available.*

3. _____ can be { divided / classified / grouped / categorized } into { three categories / two groups / three types / several kinds } according to _____: _____.

Examples:

News articles **can be** *divided* **into** *three types* **according to** *location: local, national, and international.*

Learning styles **can be** *classified* **into** *three types* **according to** *how a person takes in information: visual, auditory, and kinesthetic.*

WRITER'S TIP: Thesis Statements for Division and Classification Essays

The thesis statement of a classification essay often has three parts: the topic, the basis of classification, and the names of the groups. The basis of classification is the controlling idea: It determines how you will analyze the topic.

Circle the topic of each thesis statement and identify the basis of division and the groups.

1. *Fuels can be classified into three groups according to the physical state in which they exist in nature: solid, liquid, and gaseous.*

   Basis of division: _____

   Groups: _____

2. *Animals can be divided into three groups according to what they eat: carnivores, herbivores, and omnivores.*

   Basis of division: _____

   Groups: _____

3. *Sports can be classified into three groups according to the number of players: individual sports, two-player sports, and team sports.*

   Basis of division: _____

   Groups: _____

4. *There are three types of muscles in our body depending on their function: cardiac, smooth, and skeletal.*

   Basis of division: _____

   Groups: _____

5. *Musical instruments can be divided into four groups depending on how they produce sound: percussion, string, brass, and wind.*

   Basis of division: _____

   Groups: _____

6. *I can classify the roommates I have had according to how considerate they are into three groups: those who are very considerate, those who are indifferent, and those who are inconsiderate.*

   Basis of division: _____

   Groups: _____

Write a thesis statement for a classification essay on each of the following essay topics. Use a variety of the sentence patterns modeled on page 118. Include a basis of classification.

1. **Topic:** Restaurants in my city

   Basis of classification: _Type of food they serve_

   Thesis Statement: _The restaurants in my city can be divided according to the_
   type of food they serve into three groups: fast-food restaurants, family-style
   restaurants, and gourmet restaurants.

2. **Topic:** Courses I have taken

   Basis of classification: _____

   Thesis Statement: _____

   _____

3. **Topic:** Successful people

   Basis of classification: _____

   Thesis Statement: _____

   _____

4. **Topic:** Friends I have had

   Basis of classification: _____

   Thesis Statement: _____

   _____

5. **Topic:** Automobile drivers

   Basis of classification: _____

   Thesis Statement: _____

   _____

6. **Topic:** Television shows

   Basis of classification: _____

   Thesis Statement: _____

   _____

ANALYZING A CLASSIFICATION ESSAY

Remember that there are often several ways to divide a subject into groups. The way you divide your topic depends on the purpose of your essay. In the essay "Types of Memory," the purpose is to describe how scientists classify three types of memory.

 A **Read the essay about the three types of memory. Underline the thesis statement and circle the transitions.**

Types of Memory

Most of the activities we perform every day depend on information we have learned and saved in our memory. Everything from talking, walking, comprehending speech, reading, and socializing depends on our memory. It is our memory that allows us to remember events from a few moments ago as well as from when we were children. It is also our memory that helps us learn new skills and form habits. Psychologists, philosophers, writers, and educators are fascinated by human memory. Among their many questions are how does the brain store memories and why do people remember some kinds of information more easily than others? Although researchers still have much to learn about human memory, most agree that memory can be divided into three types according to how information is recalled: sensory memory, short-term memory, and long-term memory.

First, information comes to us through our senses—eyes, ears, nose, etc., into our sensory memory. Depending on the sense involved, information lasts in our sensory memory for one second to a few seconds. Sensory memory allows a perception such as a visual pattern, a sound, or a touch to stay in your mind for a moment after the stimulation is over. For example, if you are listening to a lecture, you need to remember the words at the beginning of a sentence in order to understand the sentence as a whole. These words are kept in your sensory memory. Or if you snap your fingers, you will notice that the sound seems to remain for a moment and then fade. Similarly, if you look at something and then close your eyes, you will still be able to "see" it for a moment because it is in your sensory memory. Your brain has the capacity to take in a lot of information fairly accurately, but because this information is not processed very much, it won't remain in sensory memory very long. Basically, sensory memory keeps an exact copy of what you see or hear, but the information disappears very quickly unless it is transferred into your short-term memory.

A second type of memory, short-term memory (STM) is also called working memory. It refers to memories that last from about twenty seconds to a minute. Unlike sensory memory, which is kept in the exact form in which it was experienced, short-term memory has received some processing. STM has a limited capacity. Most people can remember five to nine items. More than nine items and any new information usually cancels out other items from your

STM. Most items in your STM fade fairly rapidly, but other items can be kept for longer in your STM with rehearsal. Rehearsal means repeating the information over and over again. For example, a seven-digit phone number can be kept in your STM by repeating the number until you dial it, and then the number fades as soon as you start the conversation. Repetition may also increase the chances that items in your STM will enter permanent storage in long-term memory.

Finally, there is long-term memory (LTM). Unlike short-term and sensory memories, which disappear in a brief amount of time, long-term refers to memories that can be stored for a period of hours, days, weeks, years, or longer. LTM has an almost unlimited capacity and may store information permanently. It contains everything we know about the world. For example, because of your long-term memory, you can remember how to ride a bike, read a letter, send an email, sing a song, and so on. Scientific research has proven that every time we remember something, we strengthen the connection to it. This helps us remember it even after a space of many years.

Our three types of memory—sensory, short-term, and long-term—work together to process and store information. Without our memory, we could not process sensory stimuli or access past experiences and information. Everything from understanding language, recognizing family members, finding our way to school, and even buttoning a shirt would be impossible without memory.

**The left side of the brain contains all of our thoughts,
knowledge and memories. The right side is the back-up copy.**

B **Work with a partner. Answer the following questions.**

1. What are the three types of memory?

2. What is the basis of classification?

3. What examples are used to describe each type?

ESSAY PLAN: Division and Classification

Use the following plan as a guide when you write a classification essay.

DIVISION AND CLASSIFICATION ESSAY PLAN

Introduction
1. Provide background information about the topic to be classified.
2. Explain the purpose for the classification.
3. Describe how you are going to divide the topic into groups (basis of division).
4. State the number and names of the groups.
5. Provide a clear thesis statement.

Supporting Paragraphs
1. Identify and describe one group in each supporting paragraph.
2. Explain the common characteristics of the members of each group.
3. Give examples of items in each group.

Conclusion
1. Restate the method of classification.
2. Summarize the groups.

Completing a Classification Essay

Situation 1

 You are a meteorologist. You need to write an article describing the three main groups of clouds for a science museum. Here is your introduction.

The scientific study of clouds began in 1803 when Luke Howard, a British pharmacist and amateur meteorologist, introduced the first system for classifying clouds. Although many other procedures for cloud classification have been devised over the years, Howard's system is so simple and effective that it is still in use today. It is based on the shape, distribution, and altitude of clouds. He identified ten different categories, but they are all variations of three basic cloud forms. Howard used their Latin names to identify them: *cirrus* (meaning "curl"), *stratus* ("spreading out in layers or sheets"), and *cumulus* ("a pile or heap").

**Luke Howard
(1772–1864)**

B Now you need to write the three supporting paragraphs. Here are the pictures you will use as the basis for these three paragraphs. There is a lot of information, so you will have to decide which items you want to include.

Cirrus   **Stratus**   **Cumulus**

Cirrus Clouds

- found about 5 miles (8 kilometers) above sea level
- highest of all clouds
- look white, curly, feathery, delicate, streaky, wispy, thin
- sometimes called "mares' tails" because they tend to look like the tails of horses
- move at speeds of 100 to 200 miles per hour (160 to 320 kilometers per hour), but their height makes their speed seem much slower
- made entirely of ice crystals because it is so cold at that altitude

Stratus Clouds

- found 1 to 4 miles (1.6 to 6 kilometers) above the Earth
- usually arranged in smooth, flat layers
- look like a gray sheet or blanket, but not very thick, so blue sky often shines through
- sometimes called "mackerel sky" in English because they look like the scales of a fish
- often signal that bad weather may be coming
- made of water droplets

Cumulus Clouds

- found about 1 to 4 miles (1.6 to 6 kilometers) high
- their tops may rise to great heights, making them look like rising towers
- detached, look like cauliflowers
- large masses of clouds, fluffy and dome-shaped with a flat, gray base
- usually seen in summer
- if they become too dense and vertical, they often produce heavy rain, lightning, and thunder
- sometimes called "thunderheads"
- tornadoes come from thunderheads
- made of water droplets

C Write a draft of your three supporting paragraphs on a separate piece of paper.

D Exchange drafts with a classmate. Use the checklists on pages 75 and 97. Discuss any suggestions that your partner has for revision and editing. Include the introduction and add a short conclusion. Write a title for your essay. Write the revised version of your essay.

Situation 2

A You are the principal of an elementary school. You need to write an article for new teachers describing the three main types of learners: visual learners, auditory learners, and kinesthetic learners. Work in groups to research more information on the Internet about these types of learners. Write the information on the lines provided.

1. Visual learners:
   They learn best by absorbing written information and taking notes.
   These students are usually good readers.
   They can remember information presented in charts, diagrams, and pictures.

   _____

   _____

   _____

   _____

   _____

2. Auditory learners:
   They learn mainly through listening.
   These students benefit from listening to lectures and participating in discussions.
   They would rather talk than write, and they enjoy talking about what they have heard.

   _____

   _____

   _____

   _____

   _____

3. Kinesthetic learners:
   They learn better by doing.
   Students in this group need a hands-on approach.
   They often learn better when they are moving their bodies.

   _____

   _____

   _____

   _____

   _____

B Write an article about the three types of learners. Use the following thesis statement.

Thesis Statement: _Teachers recognize there are many learning styles, but they agree that most students fall into one of these three types depending on how they process information: visual learners, auditory learners, or kinesthetic learners._

WRITING A CLASSIFICATION ESSAY

In this activity, you will practice writing an essay that classifies a topic into several groups. Follow these steps:

 Prewriting

A Choose one of the following topics to write about. On a separate piece of paper, do a prewriting activity such as clustering, freewriting, or brainstorming to generate some ideas about how to divide your topic into groups.

- types of mistakes people make when learning a second language
- types of students
- types of martial arts
- kinds of bad habits
- kinds of engineers (doctors, lawyers)
- types of athletes
- kinds of television commercials
- types of drivers
- kinds of novels
- your choice

B Using the ideas you generated in your prewriting activity, determine the most appropriate basis of division or classification. Identify the groups you will write about. Make sure your groups are separate and distinct.

C Then, on a separate piece of paper, prepare an outline of your essay that includes your thesis statement and supporting ideas.

 Writing

On a separate piece of paper, write the first draft of your essay. Refer to the essay plan on page 111 to help you write your draft. Be sure to provide some background information in the introduction and include a clear thesis statement. Organize the body of the essay so that you discuss one group in each supporting paragraph. As you write the essay, use transitional phrases such as "The first type," and "The second group," or "the last category" in the topic sentences of the body paragraphs to link them together. End with a conclusion that restates the method of classification and summarizes the groups.

Revising and Editing

A *Peer Revising.* **Exchange drafts with a classmate. Use the following worksheet as a guide for suggesting improvements in your partner's essay.**

B *Personal Revising.* **Revise your essay using the checklist on page 97.**

PEER REVISION WORKSHEET

Writer: _____ Peer Editor: _____

1. What technique did the author use in the introduction? _____

   _____

   _____

2. Was the technique effective? _____ yes _____ no

   If not, how can the introduction be improved? _____

   _____

   _____

3. Are the groups used in the classification separate and distinct? _____ yes _____ no

   If not, what is another way to classify the topic? _____

   _____

   _____

4. Did the author give an adequate description of each group? _____ yes _____ no

   If not, where is more information needed? _____

   _____

   _____

5. What are the strengths and weaknesses of the conclusion? _____

   _____

   _____

C **Use any suggestions your partner made that you agree with to improve your essay.**

D *Editing.* **Use the checklist on page 75 to edit your essay. Correct all the grammar, punctuation, capitalization, and spelling errors before you hand it in.**

GO ONLINE

1. Go online to find information about hurricanes and how they are categorized. Write an essay using this as your thesis statement:

> Hurricanes are classified into five categories based on current maximum wind speed: category 1 with winds 74–95 mph, category 2 with winds 96–110 mph, category 3 with winds of 111–130 mph, category 4 with winds of 131–155 mph, and category 5 with winds of over 155 mph.

2. Go online to find out how food groups are classified. Use the information to make an informal outline of an essay about the classification of food groups. Use the outline to write an essay about how food groups are classified.

YOU BE THE EDITOR

This paragraph has ten mistakes. Correct the mistakes and copy the revised paragraph onto another piece of paper.

Types of Consumer Products

Consumer products are usually divided into three groups, convenience, shopping, and specialty products. Each group is based on the way people buys products. Convenience products are products that a consumer needs but that he or she is not willing to spend very much time or effort shopping for. Convenience products usually inexpensive, frequently purchased items. Some common examples are bread, newspapers soda, and gasoline. Buyers spend few time planning the purchase of a convenience product. Also do not compare brands or sellers. The second group, shopping products, are those products that customers feel are worth the time and effort to compare with competing products. Furniture, refrigerators, cars, and televisions are examples of shopping products. Because these products are expected to last a long time. They are purchased less frequently than convenience products. The last group consists of specialty products. Specialty products are consumer products that the customer really wants and makes a special effort to find and buying. Buyers actually plan the purchase of a specialty product. They know what they want and will not accept a substitute. A high-tech camera, a pair of skis, and a haircut by a certain stylist are examples of specialty products. In searching for specialty products. Buyers do not compare alternatives.

This woman is buying ski boots.

ON YOUR OWN

Choose one of the following topics and write a classification essay. Make sure that your introduction states the topic, gives the basis of classification, and identifies the groups. Also, make sure that your groups are separate and distinct.

- types of magazines
- kinds of phobias
- styles of architecture
- kinds of college professors or high school teachers
- types of sports fans
- kinds of social networking sites
- your own topic

CHAPTER 7 Cause and Effect Essays

LEARNING OUTCOME   **Essay Writing:** Use the writing process to write a cause or effect essay

Most people are curious. They want to know why something happened or what happened as a result of some event or situation. When your purpose is to analyze the reasons (causes) or the results (effects) of something, you should use a *cause* or *effect* type of essay. For example, when you answer a question such as, "Why did you decide to major in biology?", you are analyzing causes. When you answer a question such as, "What effects will learning English have on my career?", you are analyzing effects. Study this chart.

FOCUS ON CAUSES (OR REASONS)	FOCUS ON EFFECTS (OR RESULTS)
Causes of air pollution	Effects of TV commercials on children
Why you chose your major	Effects of high blood pressure
Reasons for taking an online college course	Effects of peer pressure on teenagers
Why reality TV shows are popular	Effects of noise pollution
Causes for the extinction of dinosaurs	Results of climate change

"They say kids these days are overweight because we don't get enough vigorous exercise. Maybe we should chew faster!"

ANALYZING CAUSES AND EFFECTS

In academic writing, you will often need to analyze causes and/or effects. For example, in a nursing class, you might need to discuss the common causes of chronic back pain or the effects of physical therapy on patients with back pain. In a history class, you might be asked to analyze the technological causes of the Industrial Revolution or the effects of the Industrial Revolution on family life in England. In an economics class, you might be required to explain the reasons for the high inflation rate in Venezuela or the effects of the high rate of inflation on the Venezuelan middle class. In an anthropology course, you might need to explore the reasons why many of the world's languages are disappearing or the effects of their disappearance on indigenous populations.

The Language of Causes and Effects: Useful Phrases and Sentence Patterns

English has many ways to express cause-and-effect relationships. The following chart shows some of the most common ones.

TRANSITION SIGNALS THAT INDICATE A CAUSE OR EFFECT RELATIONSHIP	
Transitions	**Examples**
as a consequence of	**As a consequence of** the rain, we canceled the soccer game.
as a result of	**As a result of** the rain, we canceled the soccer game.
because	**Because** it was raining, we canceled the soccer game.
because of	**Because of** the rain, we canceled the soccer game.
consequently	It was raining. **Consequently**, we canceled the soccer game.
due to	**Due** to the rain, we canceled the soccer game.
for this reason	It was raining. **For this reason**, we canceled the soccer game.
since	**Since** it was raining, we canceled the soccer game.
so	It was raining, **so** we canceled the soccer game.
therefore	It was raining; **therefore**, we canceled the soccer game.
thus	It was raining; **thus**, we canceled the soccer game

USEFUL SENTENCE PATTERNS FOR THESIS STATEMENTS FOR CAUSE OR EFFECT ESSAY

A thesis statement for a cause/effect essay always states whether the essay focuses on causes or effects. The thesis statement often (but not always) includes a specific number of causes or effects, such as "three causes" or "four effects." A strong thesis statement can also list the causes or effects that will be examined in the essay.

The following sentence patterns are useful in writing topic sentences and thesis statements for cause or effect paragraphs and essays.

1. There are several $\begin{cases} \text{causes of} \\ \text{reasons for} \underline{\hspace{2cm}}. \\ \text{effects of} \end{cases}$

There are several causes of jet lag: travel across three or more time zones, poor sleep habits prior to travel, and poor flight conditions.

There are several bad effects of drinking too much coffee: insomnia, digestive problems, and an increase in blood pressure, anxiety, and tremors.

2. There are $\begin{cases} \text{three} \\ \text{four} \\ \text{several} \end{cases}$ main reasons (causes) why $\underline{\hspace{2cm}}$.

*There are three **main reasons why** I want to share an apartment with a roommate: more space, lower rent, companionship.*

*There are three **main reasons why** my family decided to move to a bigger city: more employment opportunities, better schools, more cultural activities.*

3. $\underline{\hspace{2cm}}$ had $\begin{cases} \text{several} \\ \text{three} \\ \text{a few} \end{cases}$ important effects on $\underline{\hspace{2cm}}$.

*My parents' divorce **had** three **important effects on** my life.*

*The new shopping center **had** several **positive effects** on our community: more job opportunities, an increase in home values, and convenient places to meet and socialize.*

PRACTICE **Write a thesis statement for each topic. Use a variety of sentence patterns.**

1. **Topic:** The effects of unemployment

   Thesis statement: _____

   _____

2. **Topic:** The reasons you decided to learn English

   Thesis statement: _____

   _____

3. **Topic:** The effects of forest fires

   Thesis statement: _____

   _____

4. **Topic:** The effects of culture shock

   Thesis statement: _____

   _____

5. **Topic:** The reasons for eating a healthy breakfast

   Thesis statement: _____

   _____

6. **Topic:** The effects of deforestation

   Thesis statement: _____

   _____

7. **Topic:** The causes of obesity in children

   Thesis statement: _____

   _____

The first diagram shows how a single cause may lead to several effects. The second diagram illustrates how several causes can lead to one effect.

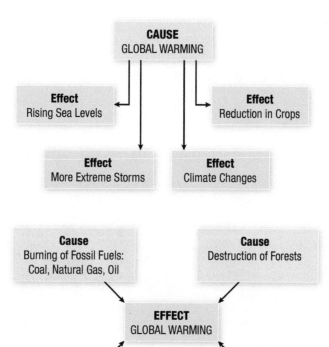

Describing Causes and Effects

Look at the news photographs here and on the next pages. Talk about them with a partner. Then write sentences about causes or effects. Use a variety of expressions from the chart on page 131.

8,000 birds, sea turtles, and marine mammals were found injured or dead after the spill.

1. a. _Many birds, turtles, and fish died because of the oil spill._

   b. _Due to the oil spill, many birds, turtles, and fish were killed or injured._

   c. _As a result of the oil spill, many birds, turtles and fish were killed or injured._

Fire causes damage and destruction to many buildings.

2. a. _____

   b. _____

   c. _____

Local man wins over $2,000,000 lottery.

3. a. _____

   b. _____

   c. _____

Heavy rain causes flood on highway and many accidents.

4. a. _____

   b. _____

   c. _____

The Duke University Blue Devils celebrate winning the school's fifth NCAA men's basketball national championship.

5. a. _____

   b. _____

   c. _____

Writing a Paragraph About Causes

Read the following conversation between two friends. Then write a paragraph that describes the reasons Janie is changing her major. Be sure to include a topic sentence and transitions. Write your paragraph on a separate piece of paper.

Mark: Hi, Janie. Have you registered for your fall classes yet?

Janie: I did it yesterday. With the improved computerized registration system, it's so much easier.

Mark: I know. I did the whole thing in ten minutes.

Janie: It took me a little longer because I've decided to change my major, and I didn't know what courses I'd need this semester.

Mark: So, you've decided not to go into anthropology after all? What happened?

Janie: I realized the job prospects weren't too good for an anthropologist with only a BA degree.

Mark: What about graduate school?

Janie: I thought about that, but I really want to start working right after graduation. Maybe I'll go to grad school in a few years, but for now I want something more practical.

Mark: I can relate to that. That's why I'm majoring in engineering. Anyway, what department are you switching to?

Janie: Believe it or not, I've decided to go into nursing. There is a big demand for nurses and great employment opportunities.

Mark: That's great, but it'll be a big change from anthropology.

Janie: I know, but I've always liked working with people and helping others. When I was in high school, I did a lot of volunteer work at the local hospital, and I found it very rewarding. I think nursing will be a very gratifying career for me.

Mark: Well, good luck with your new career choice. I guess we won't be in any of the same classes.

ANALYZING AN ESSAY ABOUT CAUSES

Ⓐ **Read the essay a student wrote about the decline of honeybees.**

Scientists are studying the causes of colony collapse disorder, which continues to kill honeybees.

Where Are the Bees?

Do you like to eat fruit such as apples, cherries, and blueberries? How about vegetables such as carrots, broccoli, and onions? These crops and hundreds of others can't grow without the help of honeybees. Why? Honeybees are responsible for pollinating more than 90 different agricultural crops. Pollination is the process of transferring pollen from one part of a plant to another, allowing plants to reproduce. Because most plants can't transfer their pollen alone, we rely on bees to make sure the food we eat continues to grow. However, over the past decade scientists have noticed that bee populations across the globe are rapidly declining. For example, the number of bees in Britain has fallen significantly in the past several years. Similarly, the United States, France, Greece, and many other countries have also suffered heavy losses in bee colonies. This situation is called colony collapse disorder (CCD). The increase of CCD is a huge problem because without bees we would not be able to eat much of the food that makes up our daily diet. Although there does not seem to be one single cause for CCD, scientists have identified three factors that are contributing to this alarming situation: parasites, pesticides, and climate change.

Scientists believe that certain parasites may be one of the major causes of colony collapse disorder. Varroa mite is an example of a parasite that kills honeybees and destroys honeybee populations. Varroa mites attach themselves to honeybees, weakening and eventually killing them by slowly sucking their blood. After testing many of the colonies affected by CCD, scientists found evidence of this parasite. Varroa mites also weaken honeybees' immune systems, leaving them in danger of infection and disease. Scientists have also identified other microscopic parasites that interfere with the honeybee's ability to breathe and fly.

The use of pesticides for pest control on crops may be another cause of CCD. Pesticides have had the unwelcome side effect of killing the bees necessary for maintaining the crops. Some pesticides farmers use to kill insects that feed on the crops we eat are poisonous. Scientists believe that when bees pollinate crops that have been sprayed with chemicals, they eat some of the pesticides as well. Because these pesticides are so strong and deadly, they may be killing not only the unwanted pests but also harming the bees. For example, some pesticides may cause bees to lose their sense of navigation. Infected bees leave their hives but are unable to find their way back home.

In addition to parasites and disease, climate change is another factor that is blamed for the decline of bee populations. Some scientists believe that warmer winters and wetter summers are the problems. The increase in global temperatures sets off a chain reaction throughout entire ecosystems. Unpredictable weather patterns lead to warm winters, drought, and floods. All of these disturbances in usual climate patterns affect flowering plants. For example, some plants may blossom early, before honeybees can fly. Other plants may not produce any flowers at all, which limits honey and pollen supplies.

Overall, CCD remains a mystery to farmers, beekeepers, and scientists around the world. Most people do not think that there is a single factor causing the death of honeybee populations. Scientists tend to believe that CCD is caused by a combination of several factors. However, one thing we can all agree on is that bees are crucial to the health of the planet and that, without them, life as we know it would drastically change. CCD could have a major impact on the quality of our food supply as well as on the price we pay for our favorite fruits and vegetables at the grocery store.

B **Work with a partner. Answer the following questions.**

1. What three main causes does the author give for CCD?

_____

_____

2. What techniques are used in the introduction and conclusion?

_____

_____

3. What cause or effect transitions did the author use to connect the ideas in the essay? Underline them.

Analyzing an Essay About Effects

A Read the essay a student wrote about the effects of the printing press.

Impact of the Printing Press

Many people consider Johannes Gutenberg's invention of the printing press to be one of the most important events in history. Before Gutenberg invented the printing press in 1440, books were copied by hand. The process was very slow, and it often took more than a year for each book to be copied. It was also very expensive. In addition, the people responsible for copying the books often made mistakes. Because of the cost and time involved in copying books, very few books were published. Those that were published were available only to monks and scholars. The invention of the printing press changed all of that. There were approximately 30,000 books in all of Europe before Gutenberg invented his printing press. Only 50 years later, there were as many as 10 to 12 million books. The invention of the printing press had several significant effects on society: bookmaking became cheaper and faster, scholars had better access to one another's ideas, regional languages increased as the use of Latin decreased.

The immediate effect of the printing press was to make bookmaking cheaper and faster. This caused an increase in the number of books published. Since books were cheaper and easier to produce, information became available to a much bigger portion of the population. Because more people had access to books, literacy increased. In the decades before the arrival of the printing press, most people around the world were illiterate and only about 30 percent of European adults could read and write. In just 200 years after Gutenberg's invention, the literacy rate increased to about 47 percent, and in the following two centuries the literacy rate reached 62 percent.

Another significant effect of the printing press was to advance science and scholarship. The printing press spurred an "information revolution" similar to the impact the Internet has today. The printing press gave scientists and scholars access to one another's work. Because the printing press enabled the spread of knowledge, new scientific discoveries were quickly shared. Before this, the only way for scientists to share their ideas was through handwritten letters or through the long and expensive process of having a book copied by hand. Mistakes were often made in the information that was copied. With the invention of the printing press, scholars and scientists were able to publish their findings quickly and accurately.

In addition, the printing press caused a decline in the use of Latin and an increase in the use of other regional languages. Before the invention of the printing press, most books were written in Latin, which was considered the language of scholarship. Unfortunately, only the most educated people could understand Latin. However, once the printing press became available to bookmakers, they printed fewer and fewer books in Latin. Soon printers started publishing books in Europe's local languages rather than in Latin. These were the everyday languages people spoke such as German, Italian, French, and English. Those who could now afford to buy books wanted them written in their own languages. They also wanted a greater variety of books, not just religious books. Almanacs, travel books, romances, and poetry were all published in local languages.

The invention of the printing press resulted in many more books being produced, and a steady rise in literacy. Printed texts became an easy way to spread information to many people quickly and cheaply. In the next fifty years, the number of books grew dramatically. Gutenberg's invention of the printing press marked an important turning point in history because it led to greater access to knowledge among a large number of people. As you can see, when Gutenberg invented the printing press, he changed the lives of people in Europe and eventually the lives of people all over the world forever.

B **Work with a partner. Answer the following questions.**

1. What three main effects of the printing press does the author discuss?

   _____

   _____

   _____

2. What techniques are used in the introduction and conclusion?

   _____

   _____

3. What cause or effect transitions did the author use to connect the ideas in the essay? Underline them.

Essay Plan: Cause or Effect

Use the following plan as a guide when you write a cause or effect essay.

CAUSE OR EFFECT ESSAY PLAN

Introduction
1. Provide background information about the situation you are analyzing.
2. Describe the situation.
3. State whether you plan to discuss its causes or its effects.
4. Identify the main causes or effects.
5. Write a thesis statement that states the focus of your essay.

Supporting Paragraphs
1. State the first (second, third) cause or effect in the first (second, third) paragraph.
2. Support the first (second, third) cause or effect with facts, examples, statistics, or quotations.

Conclusion
1. Summarize the main causes or effects.
2. Draw a conclusion or make a prediction.

WRITER'S TIP: Ordering Supporting Paragraphs

When you write an essay, you must think about how you are going to order the supporting paragraphs. Which paragraph should come first, second, and third? One common way is to organize the paragraphs according to order of importance. For example, in an essay about causes, you can begin with the most important cause and end with the least important cause. You could also begin with the least important cause and save the most important cause for last.

WRITING ESSAYS ABOUT CAUSES

Situation 1

You are a reporter for a health magazine. Your assignment is to write an article on the topic of *the causes of heart disease*.

 Prewriting

Read the assignment and discuss it with a partner.

You have just conducted an interview with a cardiologist, Dr. Harvey Snyder, and have written the following introduction:

Heart disease affects so many people that it has become a serious concern for medical science. The heart is a complex organ that is at risk to hereditary as well as environmental factors. Cardiologists think of these risk factors as either major or minor causes of heart disease.

Dr. Snyder has identified a number of risk factors associated with heart disease. He has grouped these risk factors into major and minor causes. Here are your notes from the interview:

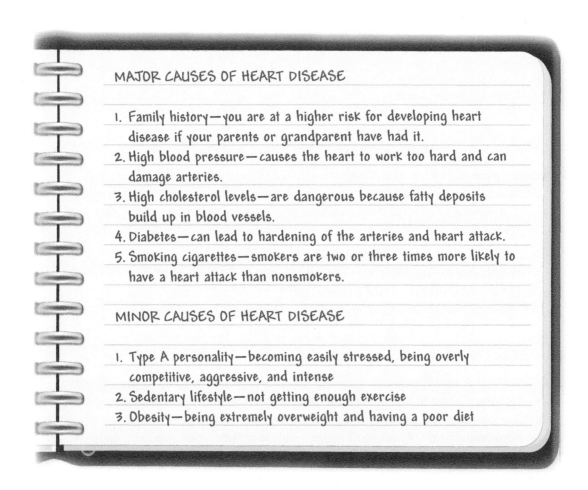

MAJOR CAUSES OF HEART DISEASE

1. Family history—you are at a higher risk for developing heart disease if your parents or grandparent have had it.
2. High blood pressure—causes the heart to work too hard and can damage arteries.
3. High cholesterol levels—are dangerous because fatty deposits build up in blood vessels.
4. Diabetes—can lead to hardening of the arteries and heart attack.
5. Smoking cigarettes—smokers are two or three times more likely to have a heart attack than nonsmokers.

MINOR CAUSES OF HEART DISEASE

1. Type A personality—becoming easily stressed, being overly competitive, aggressive, and intense
2. Sedentary lifestyle—not getting enough exercise
3. Obesity—being extremely overweight and having a poor diet

Writing

On a separate piece of paper, write a draft of two supporting paragraphs. Discuss the major causes of heart disease in one paragraph and the minor causes in the other paragraph. Also write a conclusion for your article. You might suggest ways to lessen the risks of heart disease, such as adopting a healthful lifestyle and good personal habits. Then rewrite your entire article, including the introduction, body, and conclusion, on another sheet of paper.

Revising and Editing

Exchange drafts with a partner. Use the checklists on pages 97 and 75. Discuss any suggestions that your partner has for revision and editing. Make sure that your partner has provided enough support for each cause and has connected ideas with transitions. Write a revised draft of your essay.

Situation 2

You are taking an introductory business course. You have been asked to analyze the following case and determine *the causes for the failure of a restaurant called the Undergrad Grill.*

Prewriting

 A **In small groups, read and discuss the case. Look at the drawing of Restaurant Row and the menu for the Undergrad Grill.**

CASE 8

On April 15, Tom Higgins opened a new restaurant at Benson University. He called it the Undergrad Grill. Tom had wanted to open a restaurant at Benson for several months but was waiting for the right location to become available. He was very pleased when he was able to rent suitable space on Restaurant Row. He figured that this would be a great location and worth the high rent and all the improvements he needed to make on the building. Since he wanted to open the restaurant as soon as possible, he hired the first people he could find to make the improvements on the building. He ended up overpaying the workers because he wanted to get the job done as quickly as possible. When the time came to open, he didn't have enough money to do much advertising. However, since his restaurant was surrounded by many other restaurants and since more than 25,000 undergraduate and graduate students were looking for a place to eat, Higgins was certain his restaurant would do well even without advertising. After placing several help-wanted ads in the local newspaper, Higgins hired two servers to work for him. He couldn't afford professional cooks, so he hired several students to do the cooking.

Unfortunately for Higgins, the competition was more intense than he had anticipated. After two months, his restaurant was doing poorly. One of his servers quit, and the number of customers was decreasing.

UNDERGRAD GRILL

OPEN 11 A.M. TO 8 P.M.

SOUPS

HOT & SOUR	$ 5.00
BLACK BEAN	$ 5.00
FRENCH ONION	$ 5.00
WONTON	$ 5.00
VEGETABLE	$ 5.00

DRINKS

LEMONADE	$ 4.00
COFFEE	$ 3.00
TEA	$ 3.00
SODA	$ 2.00

ENTRÉES

HAMBURGER	$ 9.95
CHEESEBURGER	$11.95
FRIED CHICKEN	$10.95
FILET OF FISH	$ 7.95
CHICKEN FAJITA	$ 9.95
BEEF FAJITA	$11.95
SHRIMP TEMPURA	$11.95
PORK FRIED RICE	$ 7.95
STEAK AU POIVRE	$12.95
SPAGHETTI & MEATBALLS	$ 8.95
CHICKEN & HUMMUS	$ 9.95
LAMB CURRY	$14.95

VEGETABLES & SIDE DISHES

BAKED POTATO	$ 4.00
FRENCH FRIES	$ 4.00
RICE	$ 4.00
CORN ON THE COB (IN SEASON)	$ 4.00
PEAS	$ 4.00
GREEN BEANS	$ 4.00
HOUSE SALAD	$ 5.50

DESSERTS

HOMEMADE APPLE PIE	$ 6.00
CHOCOLATE MOUSSE	$ 6.00
FLAN	$ 6.00
ICE CREAM	$ 5.00
MIXED FRESH FRUIT	$ 4.50

CASH ONLY
WE DO NOT ACCEPT CREDIT CARDS OR CHECKS.
NO TAKE-OUT

B Talk about why you think the restaurant did poorly. Make a list of the causes of the restaurant's failure.

1. _____

2. _____

3. _____

4. _____

5. _____

6. _____

 ## Writing

Work independently. Use your list to write an essay about the reasons (causes) the Undergrad Grill did poorly.

Revising and Editing

Revise your essay using the Revising Checklist on page 97 and the Editing Checklist on page 75. Also, check to make sure that you have provided enough support to fully describe each cause. Write a revised version of your essay.

WRITING AN ESSAY ABOUT EFFECTS

In this activity, you will practice writing an essay about effects. Follow the steps below.

Prewriting

A **Choose one of the following topics and do a prewriting activity such as clustering, freewriting, or brainstorming to generate some ideas.**

- the effects of divorce on family life
- the effects of a natural disaster such as an earthquake or hurricane
- the effects of climate on lifestyle
- the effects of a social, political, or economic problem in a country you are familiar with
- the effects that your peers have had on you
- the effects of the Internet on children
- the effects of social media on young people
- the effects of regular exercise

B **Using the ideas you generated in your prewriting, identify several major effects. Write your effects on the following lines.**

_____

_____

_____

_____

_____

_____

C **Prepare an outline for your essay on a separate piece of paper.**

Writing

On a separate piece of paper, write the first draft of your essay. Use the essay plan on page 141 to help you write your draft. Be sure to provide some background information about your topic in the introduction and include a clear thesis statement that states its main effects. Organize the body paragraphs according to order of importance, with the most important effect last. End with a conclusion that summarizes the main effects, draws a conclusion, or makes a prediction.

Revising and Editing

A *Personal Revising.* **Wait at least one day and then revise your essay using the checklist on page 97. Also, check to make sure that you have provided enough support to fully describe each effect. Write a revised version of your essay on a separate piece of paper.**

B *Peer Revising.* **Exchange drafts with a classmate. Use the following worksheet as a guide for suggesting improvements in your partner's essay.**

PEER REVISION WORKSHEET

Writer: _____   Peer Editor: _____

1. Does the introduction provide enough background information
   to interest you in the topic?   _____ yes _____ no

   If not, how can it be improved? _____

   _____

   _____

2. Are the paragraphs arranged in a logical order within the essay?   _____ yes _____ no

   If not, how can the order be improved? _____

   _____

   _____

3. Does each body paragraph provide enough support for each effect?   _____ yes _____ no

4. Are the sentences arranged in a logical order within each
   body paragraph?   _____ yes _____ no

   If not, how can the order be improved? _____

   _____

   _____

5. What are the strengths and weaknesses of the conclusion? _____

   _____

   _____

C **Incorporate any suggestions your partner has made that you agree with.**

D *Editing.* **Use the checklist on page 75 to edit your essay. Correct all the grammar,
punctuation, capitalization, and spelling errors before you rewrite it and hand it in.**

GO ONLINE

**Choose an important historical event in the history of your country. Go online to find the causes
or effects of the event. Make a list and share the information you gather with your classmates.
Then write an essay based on your research.**

YOU BE THE EDITOR

This paragraph has twelve mistakes. Correct the mistakes and copy the revised paragraph on another piece of paper.

The Great Depression of the 1930s affected the United States for generations. The collapse of the stock market began on October 24 1929, when 13 million shares of stock were sold. On October 29, known as Black Tuesday, 16 million shares were sold. The value of most shares fell sharply, resulting in financial ruin for many and widespread panic. Although there have been other financial panics. None had such a devastating effect as the Great Depression. By 1932, the industrial output of the United States had been cut in half. About 15 million people, was out of work; and salaries dropped almost 50 percent. In addition, hundreds of banks will fail. Prices for agricultural products dropped drastically. Over 90,000 businesses failed complete. Statistics, however, cannot tell the story of the hardships the masses of people suffered. For nearly every unemployed people, there were dependents who needed food and housing. People in the United States had never known such poverty and hunger before. Former millionaires stood on street corners selling apples for 5 cents. Thousands of people lose their homes. Because they could not pay there mortgages. Some people moved in with relatives. Others built shelters from tin cans and cardboard. Homeless people slept outside under newspapers. Countless people waited in lines in every city, hoping for something to eat. Unfortunately, many died of malnutrition. In 1931, more than 20,000 people committed suicide.

ON YOUR OWN

Choose one of the following general subjects and brainstorm a list of its causes or effects. Then use the ideas to write an essay.

- moving to a new country
- the explosion of the Internet
- getting good grades
- getting married or divorced
- the success or failure of a company

CHAPTER 8 Comparison and Contrast Essays

....
LEARNING OUTCOME **Essay Writing:** Use the writing process to write a comparison and contrast essay
....

Very often you will need to write about how ideas, people, or things are similar or different. In these cases, you will use a *comparison* or *contrast* type of essay. In a comparison essay, you write about the similarities, and in a contrast essay, you write about the differences.

Copyright 2013 by Randy Glasbergen.
Distributed by creators.com

**"Diet pizza is the same as regular pizza,
but you have them deliver it to
the wrong address.**

WRITER'S TIP: Choosing a Topic

When you choose a topic, make sure the two things you compare or contrast have some elements in common. For example, you could choose to compare or contrast two teachers, two movies, two types of transportation, or two computer programs. However, you would not want to compare or contrast the weather in Toronto with the nightlife in Tokyo. Instead, you could compare or contrast the weather (or the nightlife) in Toronto and the weather (or nightlife) in Tokyo. You could also compare/contrast two medical professions, for example, nurse practitioners and physician assistants. Or you could compare/contrast two team sports, such as soccer and basketball.

SHOWING THE SIMILARITIES AND DIFFERENCES

In academic writing, comparison and contrast essays are often used to support a point or persuade the reader. For example, in a history class, you might compare or contrast two leaders in order to show which one was more successful at bringing about economic reforms. In a literature class, you might compare or contrast two short stories to show which one you liked better. In an engineering class, you might compare and contrast solar energy with wind energy to explain why one is more efficient than the other.

The Language of Comparison and Contrast: Useful Phrases and Sentence Patterns

There are many ways to express similarities and differences. Study these charts, which show the most common sentence patterns for comparison and contrast.

TRANSITION SIGNALS THAT INDICATE A COMPARISON	
alike	My parents and my husband's parents are **alike** in several ways.
and . . . too	Dublin has an international airport, **and** London does, **too**.
as . . . as	The Tower's apartments are **as** expensive **as** the Park Lane's.
both . . . and	**Both** Egypt **and** Kenya are in Africa.
like	The weather in Philadelphia is **like** the weather in my hometown.
likewise	Toyota makes fuel-efficient cars. **Likewise**, Fiat makes fuel-efficient cars.
similar to	The menu at Gino's is **similar to** the menu at Frank's.
similarly	Martha has two children and works full-time. **Similarly**, Lelia is a working mother.
the same	My roommate and I like **the same** kind of music.
the same as	The altitude of Calcutta is **the same as** the altitude of Copenhagen.

TRANSITION SIGNALS THAT INDICATE A CONTRAST	
although	**Although** the Sahara Desert has a dry climate, some crops can be grown there.
but	The Sahara desert has a dry climate, **but** the Amazon Rain Forest has a wet climate.
different from	The climate in the Sahara desert is very **different from** the climate in the Amazon Rain Forest.
even though	**Even though** the Sahara Desert has a dry climate, some crops can be grown there.
however	The Sahara Desert has a dry climate. **However**, the Amazon Rain Forest has a wet climate.
in contrast	The Sahara Desert has a dry climate. **In contrast**, the Amazon Rain Forest has a wet climate.
on the other hand	The Sahara Desert has a dry climate. **On the other hand**, the Amazon Rain Forest has a wet climate.
unlike	**Unlike** rain forests, deserts get very little rain.
whereas	**Whereas** the Sahara Desert is dry, the Amazon Rain Forest is wet.
while	**While** the Sahara Desert is dry, the Amazon Rain Forest is wet.

The following sentence patterns are useful in writing topic sentences and thesis statements for comparison and contrast essays and paragraphs:

1. There are several $\begin{cases} \text{differences} \\ \text{similarities} \end{cases}$ between _____ and _____.

   There are several differences between high school and college.

   There are several similarities between high school and college.

2. _____ and _____ are $\begin{cases} \text{similar} \\ \text{different} \end{cases}$ in many ways.

   Thai food and Vietnamese food are similar in many ways.

   Thai food and Vietnamese food are different in many ways.

3. _____ is $\begin{cases} \text{different from} \\ \text{similar to} \end{cases}$ _____ in many ways.

   My father is different from his older brother in many ways.

   My father is similar to his older brother in many ways.

4. _____ and _____ have $\begin{cases} \text{several} \\ \text{many} \end{cases}$ things in common.

   My best friend and I have several things in common.

   Nurse practitioners and physician assistants have many things in common.

5. A comparison between _____ and _____ $\begin{cases} \text{reveals} \\ \text{shows} \\ \text{demonstrates} \end{cases}$ _____.

   A comparison between jazz and rock 'n' roll reveals some surprising similarities.

   A comparison between jazz and rock 'n' roll demonstrates some surprising differences.

PRACTICE **Write a thesis statement for a comparison/contrast essay on each of the following topics. Use a variety of the preceding sentence patterns.**

1. **Topic:** Working for a large corporation and working for a small company

   Thesis Statement: _____

2. **Topic:** Soccer and basketball

   Thesis Statement: _____

3. **Topic:** The education system in the United States and the education system in your country or another country

   Thesis Statement: _____

4. **Topic:** Reality TV shows and scripted TV shows

   Thesis Statement: _____

5. **Topic:** Two of your classmates

   Thesis Statement: _____

6. **Topic:** Skiing and snowboarding

   Thesis Statement: _____

7. **Topic:** Modern architecture and classical architecture

   Thesis Statement: _____

8. **Topic:** Living on campus and living off campus

   Thesis Statement: _____

Examining Comparisons and Contrasts

Ⓐ **Look at the two Internet ads. Find several similarities and differences between the two apartments. Write two sentences of comparison and two sentences of contrast. Use a variety of sentence patterns and phrases from the charts and examples on pages 149 and 150.**

```
○ ○ ○                    http://ForRent.org
Home  |  Housing  |  Apartments  |  For Rent              post  |  account
```
Spring Court Apartments: Large 2-bedroom apt., 2 bathrooms, eat-in kitchen, large living room, air-conditioning, wall-to-wall carpeting. Great location on Monument Street. NO pets. $900/month, all utilities included. Call or text Mr. Toll at (315) 555–0110.

```
○ ○ ○                    http://ForRent.org
Home  |  Housing  |  Apartments  |  For Rent              post  |  account
```
Huron Towers: 10th floor—great view of river, 3 bedrooms, 2 bathrooms, modern kitchen with new appliances, fireplace in living room, hardwood floors, air-conditioning, laundry facilities, utilities NOT included. NO pets. Pool and tennis courts on premises. $1,200/month. Call or text for appointment: (315) 555–0183.

a. *The apartment in Spring Court has two bedrooms, but the apartment in Huron Towers has three bedrooms.*

b. _____

c. _____

d. _____

e. _____

B Now do the same for the next two sets of ads.

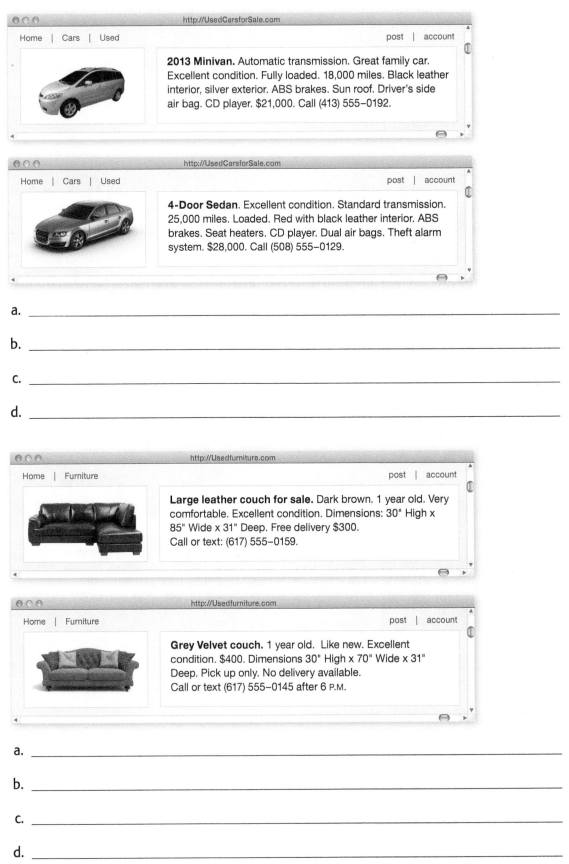

a. _____

b. _____

c. _____

d. _____

a. _____

b. _____

c. _____

d. _____

WRITING ABOUT COMPARISONS

You are studying the impact of heredity on human behavior and are researching identical twins who were separated at birth. This is the introduction you wrote for your article.

Some of the most important research in the field of behavioral genetics comes from the studies of identical twins who were separated at birth. Dr. Thomas J. Bouchard is a professor at the University of Minnesota who has conducted many important studies on identical twins. He believes that by examining their differences and similarities, we will better understand the influences of heredity and environment. One of the most interesting pairs of twins that Dr. Bouchard studied is known as "the Jim twins." Jim Springer and Jim Lewis are identical twins who were separated at birth because their fourteen-year-old mother could not take care of them. They were not reunited until thirty-nine years later. According to Dr. Bouchard, the Jim twins are "the most valuable pair that has ever been studied" because the similarities between them are so astounding.

A **Work with a partner. Discuss the list of similarities between Jim Springer and Jim Lewis. Which ones do you find the most surprising?**

- Each brother was told that his brother had died at birth.
- Both brothers are emotional, sentimental, kind, generous, friendly, and loving by nature.
- Neither brother gets angry easily, and if he does get angry, he doesn't show it.
- Both bite their fingernails and/or jiggle one foot when nervous.
- They look exactly alike.
- They are both 6 feet tall and weigh 180 pounds.
- They walk the same way.
- Both cross their legs the same way.
- Their voices sound exactly the same.
- They use the same gestures when they speak.
- Both use the same expressions, such as "Mama mía" and "Cool."
- Both enjoy woodworking and have built several birdhouses and tables.
- Both brothers are poor spellers.
- Both were married first to women named Linda.
- Their second wives were both named Betty.
- As children, they each had a dog and named it "Toy."
- They have both taken family vacations on the same beach in Florida.
- Until they were reunited, each felt as though something was missing from his life.
- Jim Springer named his son James Allen; Jim Lewis named his son James Alan.
- Both frequently buy gifts (that they cannot afford) for their wives.
- Both men have worked part-time in law enforcement.

B On a separate piece of paper, write a paragraph on the similarities between Jim Springer and Jim Lewis. Use information from the list on page 153. There are too many similarities for one paragraph. Choose the ones that you think are the most interesting to include in your paragraph. Remember to begin your paragraph with a topic sentence.

C Now revise and edit your paragraph. Give the final draft to your teacher.

METHODS OF ORGANIZATION FOR COMPARISON AND CONTRAST

There are two basic patterns for writing a comparison or contrast essay: the *block method* and the *point-by-point method*. In the block method, you describe all the similarities in the first supporting paragraph and then all the differences in the second supporting paragraph. In the point-by-point method, you identify several important points to be compared and contrasted. In the first supporting paragraph, you compare and contrast the two things according to the first point. In the second supporting paragraph, you compare and contrast the two things according to the second point, and so on. Most student writers find the block method easier to master.

Analyzing Essays of Comparison and Contrast

A Read the following two essays. The purpose of both essays is to explain why a student chose to attend Greenwell University rather than State University.

Essay 1

A Difficult Decision

Last week when I received acceptances from my top two choices for college, State and Greenwell, I knew I had a difficult decision to make. Although I had talked to friends and relatives who had attended both schools and had visited both campuses many times, I couldn't make up my mind. It was only after I analyzed the similarities and differences between the two schools that I finally came to my decision to begin classes at Greenwell in the fall.

At first glance, it seems that State and Greenwell have a lot in common. First of all, both universities are located in Pennsylvania, where I am from. The tuition is also exactly the same at both schools—$30,000 per year. In addition, the basketball team at State is just as good as the one at Greenwell, and I would love to play for either one. Most importantly, both schools have large libraries, excellent academic reputations, and first-class engineering departments.

It was when I looked at the differences between the two schools that I made my final decision. In terms of location, State is more attractive. Its setting in a safe suburb was definitely more appealing than Greenwell's location in a dangerous city neighborhood. I also liked State's older campus with its beautiful buildings and trees more than Greenwell's new campus, which looks like an office complex. But I realized that these should not be the most important factors in my decision. I had to pay a lot of attention to the financial component. Although the tuition is the same at both schools, Greenwell offered me an $8,000 scholarship, whereas State couldn't give me any financial aid. In addition, if I go to Greenwell, I can live at home and save money on room and board. Since Greenwell is much closer to home, I won't have to spend as much on transportation to and from school. The most important factor in making my decision was the difference in class size between the two universities. State has large classes and an impersonal feeling. On the other hand, Greenwell has small classes, and students get a lot of personal attention.

In conclusion, after taking everything into consideration, I think I made the right decision. Since small classes, personal attention from my professors, and saving money are all very important to me, I will probably be happier at Greenwell.

B **Work with a partner. Answer the following questions.**

1. What method of organization did the student use?

   _____

2. What is the topic sentence of the first supporting paragraph?

   _____

3. What similarities between the two schools does the author mention?

   _____

   _____

   _____

4. What is the topic sentence of the second supporting paragraph?

   _____

5. What differences between the two schools does the student mention?

   _____

   _____

   _____

Essay 2

A Difficult Decision

Last week when I received acceptances from my top two choices for college, State and Greenwell, I knew I had a difficult decision to make. Although I had talked to friends and relatives who had attended both schools and had visited both campuses many times, I couldn't make up my mind. It was only after I compared the location, cost, and quality of education of the two schools that I could finally come to my decision to attend Greenwell.

The first thing I considered was the location. First of all, both universities are located in Pennsylvania, where I am from. But that is where the similarities end. State's setting in a safe suburb is definitely more appealing than Greenwell's location in a dangerous city neighborhood. I also like State's older campus with its beautiful buildings and gardens more than Greenwell's new campus, which looks like an office complex.

In addition to location, I had to pay a lot of attention to the financial component. The tuition is the same at both schools—$30,000 per year. However, Greenwell offered me an $8,000 scholarship, but State couldn't give me any money. Also, if I go to Greenwell, I can live at home and save money on room and board. Finally, since Greenwell is much closer to home, I won't have to spend as much on transportation to and from school.

The quality of education at the two schools had the most influence on my decision. In many ways, State and Greenwell have similar standards of education. Both schools have large libraries and excellent academic reputations. Also, State has a first-class engineering department, and so does Greenwell. So I had to look at other things. What it came down to was the difference in class size between the two universities. State has large classes and an impersonal feeling. On the other hand, Greenwell has small classes, and students get a lot of personal attention.

In conclusion, after taking everything into consideration, I think I made the right decision. Since small classes, saving money, and personal attention from my professors are very important to me, I will probably be happier at Greenwell.

C **Work with a partner. Answer the following questions.**

1. What method did the author of this essay use?

_____

2. What is the thesis statement?

_____

_____

3. What three points about the schools did the author compare and contrast?

_____

_____

_____

4. How did the author organize the order of the supporting paragraphs within the essay? Least important to most important? Or most important to least important?

_____

5. What transitions did the author use to connect the ideas in the essay? Underline them.

Essay Plans: Comparison/Contrast

The information that follows summarizes what to do in each part of a comparison/contrast essay using the block format or the point-by-point format.

COMPARISON OR CONTRAST ESSAY PLAN

BLOCK FORMAT

These guidelines will help you remember what you need to do in each part of a comparison/contrast essay using the block method.

Introduction
1. Provide background information about your topic.
2. Identify the two things being compared or contrasted.
3. State the purpose for making the comparison or contrast.
4. Write a thesis statement that states the focus of your essay.

Body (Supporting Paragraphs)
1. In the first paragraph, discuss the similarities.
2. In the next paragraph, discuss the differences.

Conclusion
1. Restate the purpose for comparison and/or contrast in different words.
2. Summarize the main similarities and differences.
3. Make a conclusion.

COMPARISON OR CONTRAST ESSAY PLAN

POINT-BY-POINT FORMAT

Introduction

1. Provide background information about your topic.
2. Identify the two things being compared or contrasted.
3. State the purpose for making the comparison or contrast.
4. Identify the points to be compared or contrasted.
5. Write a thesis statement that states the focus of your essay.

Body (Supporting Paragraphs)

1. In the first paragraph, compare or contrast the two things according to the first point you identified.
2. In the second paragraph, compare or contrast the two things according to the second point you identified.
3. Do the same thing in the third and subsequent paragraphs.

Conclusion

1. Restate the purpose for comparison or contrast in different words.
2. Summarize the main similarities and differences.
3. Make a conclusion.

WRITER'S TIP: Using Point-by-Point Format

When you use the point-by-point format to write about similarities or differences, you need to decide how you are going to order the points. Again, one common way is to organize the points according to order of importance. For example, you can begin with the most important point and end with the least important point.

WRITING ESSAYS OF COMPARISON AND CONTRAST: BLOCK FORMAT

In this activity, you will practice writing an essay of comparison and contrast.

 Prewriting

A **Choose one of the following topics. On a separate piece of paper, brainstorm a list of similarities and differences.**

- Compare and contrast yourself and another member of your family.
- Compare and contrast some aspect of your culture, such as eating habits, education, government, economy, religion, or social life, with the same aspect of another culture.
- Compare and contrast a photo and a painting of the same scene.

- Compare and contrast two people you have worked with, such as two coworkers at a job, two students in a group, or two bosses you have had.
- Select your own topic.

B **Organize your list. Put the similarities in one group and the differences in another.**

SIMILARITIES	DIFFERENCES

C **Identify a purpose for making your comparison.**

For example, are you comparing two restaurants so that you can recommend one of them to a friend? Are you comparing your native language and English to show why English is easy or difficult for you to learn? Develop your essay according to your purpose.

Purpose: _____

D **Prepare an informal outline for your essay on a separate piece of paper.**

Writing

On a separate piece of paper, write the first draft of your essay. Use the essay plan for the block format on page 157 to help you write your draft. Be sure to provide some background information in the introduction and include a clear thesis statement that states your purpose for comparison. Organize the supporting paragraphs so that all the similarities are in one paragraph and all the differences are in another paragraph. End with a conclusion that restates your purpose for the comparison and that summarizes the main similarities and differences.

Revising and Editing

A *Peer Revising.* **Exchange drafts with a partner. Use the following worksheet as a guide for suggesting improvements in your partner's essay.**

PEER REVISION WORKSHEET

Writer: _____   Peer Editor: _____

1. Did the introduction identify the two items being compared?   _____ yes _____ no

2. Is the purpose of the comparison clearly stated?   _____ yes _____ no

3. Did the introduction make you want to read the rest of the essay?   _____ yes _____ no

   Why or why not? _____

   _____

4. Did the author adequately develop the points of comparison
   in a paragraph?   _____ yes _____ no

   If not, how can the paragraph be strengthened? _____

   _____

5. Did the author adequately develop the points of contrast in
   another paragraph?   _____ yes _____ no

   If not, how can the paragraph be strengthened? _____

   _____

6. Did the author include an effective conclusion? _____

   If not, how can it be improved? _____

   _____

B *Personal Revising.* **Wait at least one day and then revise your essay using the checklist on page 97. Also, check to make sure you have provided enough support to explain fully the similarities and differences. Write a revised version of your essay.**

C **Incorporate any suggestions your partner has made that you agree with.**

D *Editing.* **Use the checklist on page 75 to edit your essay. Correct all the grammar, punctuation, capitalization, and spelling errors before you write the final draft and hand it in.**

GO ONLINE

Think of something you would like to buy such as a new television, car, sewing machine, camera, piece of exercise equipment, and the like. Go online to find two examples of the product that you could purchase on the Internet. Read the descriptions of the two items and make a list of similarities and differences. For example, you can compare and contrast the price, size, quality, and features of the two items. Use the information to write a comparison or contrast essay.

YOU BE THE EDITOR

The following paragraph has ten mistakes. Correct the mistakes and copy the revised paragraph on another piece of paper.

Now that I am pregnant with our first child, my husband and I will have to find a bigger place to live. Our little apartment in the city is too small for three people. We trying to decide whether we should get a biggest apartment in the city or move to the suburbs. We have four main consideration expense, space, convenience, and schools. In general, is probably expensiver to live in the city. On the other hand, we would have to buy a car if we moved to the suburbs we would also have to buy a lawnmower and a snow blower or hire someone care for the lawn and driveway. In terms of space, we could definitely have a bigger house and much more land if we lived in the suburbs. However, we wonder if it would be worth it, since we would lose so many conveniences. Stores would be farther away, and so would friends, neighbors, movie theaters, museums, and restaurants. The most biggest inconvenience would be that we would both have to commute to work every day instead of walking or taking the bus. The schools are probably better in the suburbs, but for our child, who isn't even born yet, school is several years away. In looking at our priorities, it becomes clear that we should continue to live in the city for now and then reevaluate our decision as the baby gets closer to school age.

ON YOUR OWN

Write a comparison/contrast essay using the point-by-point method. Choose one of the following topics and identify several points on which to base your comparison. Follow the steps of the writing process as you plan, write, and revise your essay, and be sure that you have a clear purpose for your comparison.

- Compare and contrast two pieces of art or music.
- Compare and contrast communication in your generation and communication in your grandparents' generation.
- Compare and contrast two characters in a movie or book.
- Compare and contrast products that you have used such as two kinds of shampoo, two different cell phones, or two pairs of sneakers.

CHAPTER 9 ▸ Problem-Solution Essays

....
LEARNING OUTCOME   **Essay Writing:** Use the writing process to write a problem and solution essay
....

We are all constantly looking for ways to solve problems. The problem might be a personal one, such as losing weight or having trouble sleeping. Or the problem might be related to work, school, society, the economy, or politics. When your purpose is to describe a problem and suggest possible solutions, you will write a *problem-solution* essay. For example, you would write this type of essay if you are discussing solutions to the problem of employee dissatisfaction in your company or solutions to overcoming the problems of adjusting to another culture.

ANALYZING SOLUTIONS TO A PROBLEM

The problem-solution pattern is very useful in academic writing. For example, you would use it in a sociology class if you were asked to talk about solutions to the problem of illiteracy in your community. You could also write this type of essay in an economics class if you needed to suggest some ways to solve the unemployment problem in your city. In an earth science course, you would use this type of essay to write about solutions to the problem of global warming.

© Randy Glasbergen
www.glasbergen.com

GLASBERGEN

"My team has created a very innovative solution, but we're still looking for a problem to go with it."

Proposing Solutions

Work in small groups. Discuss each problem and think of three or four possible solutions. Then compare your solutions with those of your classmates.

1. Living in a foreign country can be fun and exciting, but it can also be problematic. One of the most serious problems that people living in a foreign country face is culture shock. What ways can you think of to help people deal with this problem?

   Problem: Culture shock
   Solutions:

   a. _Keep in touch with your family and friends at home._

   b. _____

   c. _____

2. Many people have trouble falling asleep or staying asleep for an adequate amount of time. This problem is known as insomnia. What suggestions would you give to people who cannot seem to get a good night's sleep?

   Problem: Insomnia
   Solutions:

   a. _____

   b. _____

   c. _____

3. The population of the world keeps growing. Every second, four babies are born. Experts predict that by the year 2050, the global population is expected to be close to 9.6 billion, up from the 7.2 billion people on Earth today. The problem is that there probably will not be enough food to feed everyone. What solutions can you come up with to help solve this problem?

   Problem: Overpopulation
   Solutions:

   a. _____

   b. _____

   c. _____

4. Many large cities around the world have high rates of crime. Is crime a serious problem in the large cities of your native country? What solutions can you think of to reduce crime?

   Problem: Crime in large cities
   Solutions:

   a. _____

   b. _____

   c. _____

5. Stress at work or school can be a serious problem. A person suffering from too much stress usually finds it difficult to be productive or happy. What are some ways to reduce the amount of stress in someone's life?

Problem: Stress at work or school
Solutions:

a. _____

b. _____

c. _____

6. Illiteracy is a serious problem all over the world. For example, 25 percent of children in the United States grow up without learning to read and write. People who cannot read and write have many disadvantages. What solutions can you come up with to help overcome this problem?

Problem: Illiteracy
Solutions:

a. _____

b. _____

c. _____

7. Many of the Earth's resources are nonrenewable and will eventually run out. In order to make our valuable natural resources last longer, we need to conserve materials and recycle them as much as possible. Unfortunately, it is not always easy to convince people of the necessity of recycling. What ideas do you have about getting people to recycle?

Problem: Getting people to recycle
Solutions:

a. _____

b. _____

c. _____

Writing Thesis Statements for a Problem-Solution Essay

PRACTICE A Read the introduction to an essay that proposes solutions to the global energy crisis. Underline the thesis statement.

Energy Sources: A Dilemma for the Twenty-first Century

All of us have come to expect that reliable sources of energy will be available forever. We drive our cars wherever and whenever we want. When the gas tank gets low, we simply pull into the nearest gas station. At home, whenever we need to change the temperature, prepare food, listen to music, or watch TV, we simply turn on the nearest appliance. What is the source of all this energy that we use so carelessly? In most of the world, energy is created by burning fossil fuels—coal, natural gas, and oil. The problem is that these resources will not last forever. At our current rate of use, by the year 2080, the world's supply of oil will be almost gone. That means that if you are under the age of forty, the day will probably come when you will not have enough gasoline for your car or electricity for your appliances. Three commonly proposed solutions to the worldwide energy problem are increasing the efficiency of appliances and vehicles, improving conservation efforts, and finding alternative energy sources.

Notice that the introduction to a problem-solution essay does several things:

- Gets your reader interested in the problem (captures the readers' attention)
- Convinces your reader that the problem is important and that it needs to be solved
- Proposes several reasonable solutions in a thesis statement

B Write a thesis statement for a problem-solution essay for each of the problems you discussed on pages 163–164. A strong thesis statement should identify the problem and list several possible solutions.

1. <u>Several ways to deal with the problem of culture shock include keeping in touch with your family and friends at home, making new friends in your host country, and keeping an open mind about new customs and food.</u>

2. _____

_____

3. _____

_____

4. _____

_____

5. _____

_____

6. _____
   _____

7. _____
   _____

Writing Topic Sentences for Supporting Paragraphs for a Problem-Solution Essay

Each supporting paragraph in the essay should begin with a topic sentence that states one solution. For example, in the essay on solutions to the energy crisis, each topic sentence identifies one solution.

Supporting paragraph 1: One solution to the energy crisis is to increase the energy efficiency of appliances and vehicles.

Supporting paragraph 2: Another solution to the critical energy situation is to improve our conservation efforts.

Supporting paragraph 3: The best solution to the energy crisis is to find alternative sources of energy to meet our future needs.

PRACTICE **Choose four of the problems you discussed on pages 163–164 and write a topic sentence for each of the supporting paragraphs.**

Problem: _____

Supporting Paragraph 1: _____

Supporting Paragraph 2: _____

Supporting Paragraph 3: _____

Problem: _____

Supporting Paragraph 1: _____

Supporting Paragraph 2: _____

Supporting Paragraph 3: _____

Problem: _____

Supporting Paragraph 1: _____

Supporting Paragraph 2: _____

Supporting Paragraph 3: _____

Problem: _____

Supporting Paragraph 1: _____

Supporting Paragraph 2: _____

Supporting Paragraph 3: _____

Offering Solutions

A You are the advice consultant for a website. How would you respond to the following emails? Be sure to offer several solutions to each problem in your response. Share your responses by exchanging papers with your classmates or by reading them out loud.

To: Adviser@internet.com
From: CR@internet.com
Subject: Career advice

Dear Adviser,

I have a big problem, and I hope you can help me solve it. I got my undergraduate degree two years ago. I majored in business because I knew that my father expected me to join him and my brother in the family business. My grandfather opened his first men's clothing store in 1975, and my father took it over and expanded it to three stores in 2000. I have worked in the marketing department for the past two years. I was never sure I wanted to join the family business, but I felt a lot of pressure from my parents to join it, and I knew that would make my parents happy. Now I realize that this work does not make me happy, and that it is not a career choice I would have made on my own. I would rather go into teaching. I'm afraid to tell my father that I want to leave the business. I'm also afraid to ask him to pay for me to go back to graduate school for a master's degree in teaching. He expects me to get my MBA like my brother. I'm really torn. I'm very close to my family and don't want to hurt their feelings, but I would rather dedicate my life to doing work I am passionate about. What advice can you give me?

Torn

Dear Confused,

_____

_____

_____

_____

_____

_____

_____

_____

To: Adviser@internet.com
From: KB@internet.com
Subject: Roommate problem

Dear Adviser,

I'm a sophomore in college. Last year my roommate, Jane, and I were very good friends. I don't know what happened, but this year everything has changed. Jane seems really different. She has a whole new group of friends and spends all of her time with them. She stays out late at night and often doesn't get up in time for her classes. She never studies any more, and she got kicked off the soccer team for missing so many practices. She's always either sleeping or out with her new friends. When she's in our room, she is moody, messy, and undependable. Please tell me what to do. I've tried talking to her, but she just tells me to mind my own business. I'm concerned that she's going to get kicked out of school. She's already on academic probation. What should I do?

Concerned

Dear Concerned,

_____

_____

_____

_____

_____

_____

_____

_____

B Work with a partner. On a separate piece of paper, write your own letter to the advice consultant. You can write about a real problem that you have or make one up. Then exchange letters with a classmate and write a response.

ANALYZING A PROBLEM-SOLUTION ESSAY

 Read the essay one student wrote that offers four solutions to the food shortage crisis.

Solving the World's Food Shortage Crisis

There is no doubt that we face a global food shortage crisis. With the price of grains such as wheat, rice, and corn rising from year to year, more people continue to go hungry. In countries such as Haiti and Bangladesh, the food shortage has become so serious that people are rioting in the streets in protest of rising food prices. Most experts agree that the food shortage problem is linked to the energy crisis that is also threatening communities worldwide. The rising cost of oil has made it more and more expensive for farmers to operate machinery that aids in mass food production. Higher oil prices also make the transport of food to people in need much more expensive. Poor farmers, who cannot afford to buy fuel, seeds, or other important agricultural tools, have begun to cut back on their own food production. In addition, many scientists believe that the climate changes have adversely affected food production by causing droughts that make it impossible for anything to grow. In order to prevent this problem from growing worse and ruining economies around the world, it is crucial that we put sensible solutions into practice. Several achievable solutions to the food shortage crisis are ending financial aid for biofuel, introducing new farming techniques, protecting farm land from bad weather, and eating less meat.

According to experts, one solution is to eliminate government policies that encourage the development of ethanol and other biofuels. In order to reduce the risk of global warming, both the United States and Europe are exploring alternative energy sources. One of the main sources that has been discovered and widely used is ethanol. However, because ethanol is made from corn, it has directly affected the food shortage by taking away corn that could be used as food for humans and animals. It is critical that governments end policies that give farmers financial breaks for converting food to fuel are suspended. Ending such policies will not only make more food available, it will also free up land now used to grow corn for biofuel so that it can be used for growing crops that feed hungry people.

Another solution is for scientists to develop new methods to increase crop production. Researchers around the world are studying ways to improve crops and farming techniques. Two such places that are making important discoveries are the International Rice Research Institute in the Philippines and the International Maize and Wheat Improvement Center in Mexico. Scientists there are growing staple crops such as wheat, rice, maize, and soy that are more resistant to pests and weeds. The new and improved crops are also more nutritious and yield higher quantities. The goal is to offer more nutrition per acre of farmed land.

In addition to increasing crop production, helping farmers protect their land against bad weather conditions is another possible solution to the global food shortage crisis. Unprepared farmers and unpredictable weather are a recipe for disaster. For example, droughts in Australia (the world's second largest wheat producer) have left hundreds of farms unproductive and even more people without food. A farm pond is one preventative method scientists have developed to combat the threat of droughts. By creating a small pond on farming land, a farmer can easily collect rainwater to use for emergency irrigation during a drought. This simple solution is a great way to increase farm productivity in areas of the world most affected by troubling weather conditions.

Governments and farmers aren't the only groups that must work towards a solution to the global food shortage crisis. Consumers, the people actually buying the food that is becoming more expensive and less available, are also responsible for helping decrease shortage. One very simple thing that all consumers can do is buy and eat less meat. Cows, chickens, and pigs are all fed with food made from corn and other important grains. The large amount of food needed to feed them before they are slaughtered could be used to feed humans if the demand for meats decreased.

There is no doubt that the global food shortage problem needs to be dealt with immediately. The only way to prevent further worldwide hunger and malnutrition is for everyone to work together to implement solutions to the problem. There are many things that governments, farmers and consumers can do to help fight the growing food shortage problem. Introducing new farming techniques, ending biofuel aid, protecting farmland, and eating less meat are a few possible solutions. There is never an excuse for people to go hungry. Hopefully, a growing awareness of the problem will be the first step to finding ways to resolve it.

B　**Work with a partner. Answer the following questions.**

1. What is the thesis statement of the essay? Underline it.

2. What four solutions to the food shortage crisis does the student propose?

_____

_____

_____

_____

3. What technique(s) does the student use in writing the conclusion?

_____

Essay Plan: Problem-Solution

Use the following plan as a guide when you write a problem-solution essay.

PROBLEM-SOLUTION ESSAY PLAN

Introduction
1. Describe the problem and state why it is serious.
2. Write a thesis statement that identifies several possible solutions.

Body (Supporting Paragraphs)
1. Discuss one solution in each supporting paragraph.
2. Provide details to explain each solution.
3. If you think one of your solutions is the best, save it for the last body paragraph. In other words, organize the paragraphs according to order of importance.

Conclusion
1. Summarize the solutions.
2. Draw a conclusion or make a prediction based on your suggestions.

Remember to use transitions between body paragraphs. The body paragraphs often start with a topic sentence that links the solution in the previous paragraph to the next solution. You may also use signals such as *in addition, another, besides, furthermore.*

WRITING PROBLEM-SOLUTION ESSAYS

Review the following case (from Chapter 7). Previously, you focused on the causes of the restaurant's failure. Now, Tom wants to reopen his restaurant and make it a success. In this activity, you will offer solutions to his problems.

CASE 8

On April 15, Tom Higgins opened a new restaurant at Benson University. He called it the Undergrad Grill. Tom had wanted to open a restaurant at Benson for several months but was waiting for the right location to become available. He was very pleased when he was able to rent suitable space on Restaurant Row. He figured that this would be a great location and well worth the high rent and all the renovations he needed to do on the building. Since he wanted to open the restaurant as soon as possible, he hired the first people he could find to do the renovations and painting. He ended up overpaying the workers because he wanted to get the job done as quickly as possible. When the time came to open, he didn't have enough money to do much advertising. However, since his restaurant was surrounded by many other restaurants and since more than 25,000 undergraduate and graduate students were looking for a place to eat, Higgins was certain his restaurant would do well even without advertising. After placing several help-wanted ads in the local newspaper, Higgins hired two servers to work for him. He couldn t afford professional cooks, so he hired several students to do the cooking.

Unfortunately for Higgins, the competition was more intense than he had anticipated. After two months, his restaurant was doing poorly. One of his servers had quit and the number of customers was decreasing.

Prewriting

Work with a partner and brainstorm a list of solutions to Tom Higgins's problem.

Solutions

_____

_____

_____

_____

_____

_____

Writing

Use your list from above to plan and write an essay that offers solutions to Tom Higgins's problem. Choose several of the solutions on your list to develop into the supporting paragraphs. Begin with an introduction that gives some background about the problem and includes a thesis statement stating the solutions you are going to discuss. Then write the supporting paragraphs using one solution for each paragraph. Finally, write a conclusion that leaves your reader thinking about the solutions.

Revising and Editing

Exchange drafts with a classmate. Discuss any suggestions that your partner has for revision and editing. Use the Revising Checklist on page 97 and the Editing Checklist on page 75. Write a revised version of your essay and hand it in.

WRITING MORE PROBLEM-SOLUTION ESSAYS

Follow these steps to write another problem-solution essay.

Prewriting

A Write a problem-solution essay based on one of the problems you analyzed in Proposing Solutions on pages 163–164. Make a list of the solutions you are going to write about here.

_____

_____

_____

_____

B Make an informal outline of the essay on another piece of paper.

Writing

Use your list from the previous page to plan and write a draft of an essay that offers solutions. Use the essay plan on page 170 to help you with your draft. Be sure to provide some background information on the problem in the introduction and include a clear thesis statement. Organize the supporting paragraphs according to order of importance, beginning or ending with the most important solution. For each supporting paragraph, include a topic sentence that states the solution. End with a conclusion that summarizes the solutions, draws a conclusion, or makes a prediction.

Revising and Editing

A *Personal Revising.* Wait at least one day and then revise your essay using the checklist on page 97. Be sure that each paragraph describes one possible solution. Also, check to make sure you have provided enough support to explain each solution fully. Write a revised version of your essay and hand it in.

B *Peer Revising.* Exchange drafts with a classmate. Use the following worksheet as a guide for suggesting improvements in your partner's essay.

PEER REVISION WORKSHEET

Writer: _____   Peer Editor: _____

1. What are some interesting things you learned from reading this essay? _____

   _____

   _____

2. Did the introduction provide enough background
   information to explain the problem?   ____ yes ____ no

3. How many solutions did the author offer in the essay? _____

   _____

   Is each solution adequately developed in a separate
   supporting paragraph?   ____ yes ____ no

4. Are the paragraphs arranged in a logical order?   ____ yes ____ no

   What type of order did the author use? _____

5. Did the author use transitions to guide you from one idea
   to the next?   ____ yes ____ no

6. Were there any irrelevant sentences that should be eliminated? ____ yes ____ no

7. Did the author include a conclusion that summarizes the
   solutions or makes a prediction?   ____ yes ____ no

C Incorporate any suggestions your classmate made that you agree with.

D *Editing.* Use the checklist on page 75 to edit your essay. Correct all the grammar, punctuation, capitalization, and spelling errors before you write the final draft.

GO ONLINE

Think of a problem you might have in your everyday life—for example, you spilled coffee on your carpet, you want to lose weight, you want to buy an out-of-print book, you are having trouble sleeping, or you want to improve your vocabulary. Go online to find several possible solutions to your problem. Write a paragraph that describes the problem and explains the solutions.

YOU BE THE EDITOR

The following article has seven mistakes. Correct the mistakes and copy the revised paragraph on another piece of paper.

If you are like most people, you average one to three colds per year. Even if you do not have a cold right now. The chances are three in four that within the next year, at least one cold virus will find you. Then you'll spend a week or so suffering from the miseries of the common cold: fatigue, sore throat, laryngitis, sneezing, stuffy or runny nose, and coughing. According to researchers, colds are the most common medical reason for missing school and work.

Once you catch a cold, what can you do. There is no known cure yet for a cold. There are, however, several thing you can do to suppress the symptom s so that you feel better while the virus runs its course. For example, make sure that you get plenty of sleep and drink lots of liquids. You may find commercially available cold remedies such as decongestants, cough suppressants, and expectorants helpful, but keep in mind that these products can cause side effects. Many people prefer home remedies such as chicken soup, garlic, and ginger tea. In treating a cold, remember the wisdom of the ages, "if you treat a cold, it will be gone in a week; if you don t treat it, will be gone in seven days."

Source: Jane Brody s Cold and Flu Fighter

These people resolved the problem of which movie to watch on television.

ON YOUR OWN

Write a problem-solution essay based on one of the following problems. Identify several possible solutions to the problem. Be sure your essay has an introduction that describes the problem, several supporting paragraphs that explain the solutions, and a conclusion that summarizes the solutions or makes a prediction.

- overcrowding in your school
- the generation gap
- an argument with a friend
- deforestation
- access to the workplace for the disabled
- drug abuse

PART 3

WRITING FOR SPECIFIC PURPOSES

In Part 1 of this book, you worked on the building blocks of good writing: prewriting and planning, developing a paragraph, organizing an essay, and revising and editing. In Part 2, you focused on the basics of typical five-paragraph essays of process, division-classification, causes and effects, comparison/contrast, and problem-solution. In Part 3, you will learn about the kinds of writing required for specific purposes such as writing summaries, expressing your opinions, and writing essays for undergraduate and graduate school applications. As you continue on the road to good writing, you will appreciate more and more the importance of matching your writing to your specific purpose.

CHAPTER 10 Writing Summaries

Paragraph Writing: Write a one-paragraph summary of an article

Writing a summary requires some special skills. Unlike many other types of writing, a summary should not include your own ideas. The purpose of a summary is to condense what another author has written. This means reducing what the author has written to its main points.

Summarizing information is an important skill. Summaries are used in every field of academics. For example, in a business class, you might summarize an article from the *Wall Street Journal.* In science classes, summaries are often used in lab reports. In a literature class, you might write summaries of novels.

SUMMARIZING AN ARTICLE

A good summary presents a clear, concise idea of the main points of an article. To write an effective summary, you need a good understanding of the original article. You need to read the article carefully to determine the author's purpose and main ideas.

Steps in Writing a Summary

The following steps will help you write an effective summary.

1. **Read the article one time quickly for general understanding.** Determine the author's main idea.

2. **Read the article again more carefully.** As you read, underline main ideas, key terms, and facts.

3. **Take notes on the article on a separate piece of paper.** Your notes will be a rough outline of the article.

4. **Using your notes as a guide, write the first draft of your summary.** It should include the following:
   a. A topic sentence that states the name of the article (including the author, if available) and the main point
   b. Supporting sentences that explain, in your own words, the main supporting ideas in the article (Try answering: *What? Where? When? Who? Why?*)
   c. A final statement that summarizes the author's conclusions

5. **Revise and edit the draft of your summary.**
   a. Make sure you have accurately summarized the author's main ideas.
   b. If you included any of the author's minor points, eliminate them.
   c. Take out any of your own thoughts or opinions about the topic.

Analyzing a One-Paragraph Summary

A Reread the article "Solving the World's Food Shortage Crisis" on pages 169–170 and complete the exercise that follows.

B Read the four summaries of the article that different students wrote. Discuss them with a partner.

Summary 1

"Solving the World's Food Shortage Crisis" discusses several solutions to the problem of food shortage. The author believes that we need to work together to overcome this crisis and that we can do many things to prevent worldwide hunger.

Summary 2

This interesting article is about the worldwide food shortage crisis and ways we can eliminate the problem. It's about time that we made the food shortage crisis one of our top concerns. How can we overcome this pressing problem? The author describes several ways. Scientists are looking for ways to improve crops and farming methods. Some discoveries are being made at the International Rice Research Institute in the Philippines. Other discoveries are coming from the International Maize and Wheat Center in Mexico. I hope that in the not too distant future, people everywhere will try to prevent an even bigger food shortage crisis.

Summary 3

In "Solving the World's Food Shortage Crisis," the author describes several possible ways to eliminate the growing problem of world hunger caused by the energy crisis and climate change. Four specific solutions that governments, farmers, and consumers can implement are offered and explained: ending financial aid for biofuel, introducing new farming techniques, protecting farm land from bad weather, and eating less meat. The author hopes that as more people become aware of the problem, steps to solve it will be found.

Summary 4

The article talks about the food shortage crisis by describing the causes of the problem and outlining several ways we can solve the problem. According to the article, the energy crisis and climate change are causing the crisis. Although the population explosion is another cause, the article does not mention it. The author outlines several important ways to address the problem. All of the suggestions are good, but some other solutions should have been included. I think this article has a lot of good ideas about how to solve the global food shortage, but should have provided information about improving food aid programs.

Which summary do you think is the best? Why?

_____

_____

_____

C Analyze the other three summaries and determine what kinds of mistakes the students made. Write the summary number and briefly describe the mistakes.

Summary: _____

Mistakes: _____

_____

_____

Summary: _____

Mistakes: _____

_____

_____

Summary: _____

Mistakes: _____

_____

_____

© Randy Glasbergen
glasbergen.com

"I love reading. I read about 3 hours a day.
My favorite book is Facebook."

Completing a One-Paragraph Summary

Pretend you are doing research on sleep. You found a magazine article that suggests a new theory about why animals sleep. Read the article "The New Theory about Why Animals Sleep" and complete the summary that follows.

The New Theory about Why Animals Sleep: To Maintain the Immune System

New study shows that mammals that sleep more have more immune cells and fewer parasites.

by Amy Barth

Why do we sleep? An international team of researchers recently published evidence that slumber may have evolved to protect animals from disease. They examined sleep patterns of more than 30 mammalian species—including hedgehogs, baboons, seals, and elephants—along with the strengths of their immune systems and levels of parasite infection. Some animals, such as giraffes, doze for just a few hours a day; others, such as armadillos, snooze for 20 hours.

The study found that animals that sleep the longest had six times as many immune cells as those that take short siestas. Additionally, critters catching the fewest z's had 24 times as many parasites as the best-rested species.

"Maintaining the immune system may be the reason sleep has evolved," says lead researcher Brian Preston, an evolutionary ecologist at the Max Planck Institute for Evolutionary Anthropology in Germany.

Other scientists note that boosting the body's defenses is just one of many vital functions of sleep. It also allows the brain to reorganize connections between neurons, consolidate memories, and synthesize proteins and cholesterols that are important in tissue repair, says Allan Pack, director of the University of Pennsylvania Center for Sleep.

Another new study bolsters the link between sleep and immune function in humans. Among 153 people voluntarily infected with a cold virus, those who averaged fewer than seven hours of sleep each night were nearly three times more likely to get sick than those with eight hours or more. "We've barely scratched the surface when it comes to understanding the health implications of sleep," Preston says, "but it's clear we should all get a good night's rest."

Discover, April 2009

In "The New Theory about Why Animals Sleep" by Amy Barth, _____

_____ reported evidence that suggests _____

_____. The scientists studied

_____. They discovered that animals

that slept _____ while animals that slept

_____. According to researcher Brian

Preston, _____.

WRITING ONE-PARAGRAPH SUMMARIES

 Prewriting

A **Read the article "A Chimp off the Old Block" once to determine the main idea.**

The chimp prodigy Ayumu demonstrates his literary skills by matching Japanese characters to colored shapes on a computer screen. Ai, a 25-year-old chimpanzee, is something of a celebrity due to her mental prowess. At the Kyoto University Primate Research Institute in Japan, she has learned to read several dozen characters in *kanji*, a form of written Japanese. Still, researchers were taken aback in February when they discovered that Ai's young son, Ayumu, may be teaching himself how to read.

A Chimp off the Old Block by Curtis Rist

Ai spends part of each day at a computer monitor, where she likes to match written words to colors and shapes so that she can earn 100-yen coins to buy snacks. On February 16, when only a video camera was watching, 10-month-old Ayumu jumped up to the monitor and correctly matched the kanji word for brown with a brown square. "It was astonishing," says Tetsuro Matsuzawa, a primatologist at the institute. "He had never even touched the screen before." Researchers are now hopeful that Ayumu will continue to learn simply by observing his mother, without having to be coached.

So what did the precocious primate do with the 100 yen earned for making his first word match? "He bought some raisins from our vending machine," says Matsuzawa. "They're his favorite."

Discover, January 2002
Photograph by Tony Law

B **Write the main idea.** _____

_____

C Read the article again and take notes on the important points. _____

_____

_____

_____

_____

_____

Writing

Write a first draft of your summary. Include only the main points of the article. Try to answer the following questions: *What? Where? When? Who?* **and** *Why?*

_____

_____

_____

_____

WRITER'S TIP: Use Your Own Words

Remember to use your own words when you write a summary, but do not include your own ideas.

Revising and Editing

A *Peer Revising.* **Exchange papers with a partner. Use the following worksheet as a guide for suggesting improvements in your partner's summary.**

PEER REVISION WORKSHEET

Writer: _____   Peer Editor: _____

1. Does the summary begin with a sentence that states the
   name and main idea of the article?   _____ yes _____ no

2. Does the summary present the main supporting points?   _____ yes _____ no

3. Was the writer careful not to include any minor details
   or personal opinions?   _____ yes _____ no

4. Does the summary end with a statement that summarizes
   the author's conclusion?   _____ yes _____ no

B **Incorporate any suggestions your classmate has made that you agree with.**

C *Personal Revising.* **Revise your essay using the checklist on page 97. Write a revised version of your essay to hand in.**

D *Editing.* Use the checklist on page 75 to edit your summary. Correct all the grammar, punctuation, capitalization, and spelling errors before you hand it in.

WRITING MORE SUMMARIES

A Read the following article once to determine the main idea.

Politics as Usual
by Diana Childress

When polio paralyzed Franklin Roosevelt in August 1921, he put on a brave front. Having learned from childhood to bear pain "without fuss," he joked about a thirty-nine-year-old man getting a baby's disease and radiated optimism about his recovery. "The doctors say," he wrote a friend in December, "that by this Spring I will be walking without any limp."

But as Franklin's wife, Eleanor, said later, "I know that he had real fear when he was first taken ill." Polio was "a trial by fire." A big question in everyone's mind was how this crippling blow would affect Franklin's future in politics.

For Sara Roosevelt, the answer was perfectly clear. Her son, she felt, had already served his country well. With her money to support him, he could retire to the family home in Hyde Park and enjoy his business interests and hobbies.

Sara's views were typical of the times. In the early 1900s, people with physical disabilities were treated like invalids, either hospitalized or kept at home. Many thought it "bad manners" for a disabled person to appear in public. The idea of a "cripple" pursuing a political career was unthinkable.

Eleanor also doubted that her husband could ever return to public office. But she knew how important Franklin's political ambitions were to him. The doctors told her that keeping hope alive would improve his chances of recovery. Taking an active part in life, even if it tired him, was "better for his condition," they said. So she encouraged and helped him to stay involved in politics.

Louis Howe, Franklin's longtime political adviser, added his support. Within days after falling ill, Franklin was dictating letters that he could not even sign because the paralysis had temporarily spread to his arms and thumbs. He agreed to become a member of the executive committee of the Democratic party in New York State even though at that time, as one biographer notes, he was lying in bed and "working for hours to try to wiggle a big toe."

With Howe's help, Franklin kept the general public from finding out how seriously ill he was. Meanwhile, he worked feverishly to try to regain the use of his legs. Determined to make a full recovery, he spent much of his time exercising and struggling to learn to walk. When Democratic leaders urged him to run for U.S. senator or governor of New York in 1922, he had to admit he was not ready. Yet he kept busy on the sidelines, writing letters and articles while Howe and Eleanor appeared for him in public.

In 1924, Franklin could not avoid the Democratic National Convention and still be taken seriously as a politician. The agile man who had vaulted over a row of chairs to reach the speaker's platform in 1920 now inched painfully forward on crutches. "But nothing was the matter with his voice or his enthusiasm," wrote a reporter. His half-hour speech nominating Al Smith for president was cheered for an hour and thirteen minutes.

Four years later, Franklin still hoped that another year or two of rehabilitation would free him from his wheelchair and crutches. He tried to avoid the calls from the New York State Democratic Convention urging him to accept the nomination for governor. But when the Democratic presidential candidate, Al Smith, finally got him on the line, he realized he could no longer plead illness without letting his party down.

Franklin Roosevelt's return to active politics in spite of his inability to walk was a major triumph for himself and for disabled people everywhere. He never achieved full recovery, but his years of hard work brought a maturity and a depth of understanding that enhanced his greatness as a leader.

B Reread the article and take notes on the important points.

_____

_____

_____

_____

_____

C Use your notes to write a one-paragraph summary of the article on a separate piece of paper.

D Revise and edit your summary before you hand it in.

E   Read the following article. Follow the steps for writing a summary. Then on a separate piece of paper, write a one-paragraph summary of the article.

The Extinction of the Dinosaurs
by Daniel Lourie

For almost 140 million years, dinosaurs and other large reptiles ruled the land, sky, and sea. Dinosaurs came in sizes and shapes suited to every corner of the world. This time in the Earth's history is called the Cretaceous period. Then, approximately 65 million years ago, these huge reptiles died out and mammals took over the Earth. Few mysteries have puzzled scientists as much as this great extinction that killed off all the dinosaurs. Over the years, scientists have developed many theories to explain the disappearance of the dinosaurs. Three possible reasons are a change in the Earth's climate, disease, and the Earth's collision with a large asteroid.

Some scientists believe that a change in the Earth's climate caused the number of dinosaurs to decline and eventually disappear. During the Cretaceous period, the climate was tropical. Research indicates that at the end of the Cretaceous period, the temperature dropped and the climate became much colder. Many kinds of dinosaurs could not survive in the colder climate. Also, many of the plants that the plant-eating dinosaurs ate died. Many of the plant-eating dinosaurs died because they had nothing to eat. As the plant-eating dinosaurs died off, so did the meat-eating dinosaurs that ate them. The colder climate may have caused problems for the dinosaurs in other ways, too. Because of their size, many dinosaurs were too big to hibernate in dens. They also lacked fur or feathers for protection against the cold. As a result, the dinosaurs were unable to adapt to the new cold conditions.

Another possible reason that dinosaurs became extinct is disease. Some scientists think that diseases killed off the dinosaurs when large groups migrated across newly created land bridges between the separate continents. For example, land bridges opened up between Asia and North America, allowing species of dinosaurs to travel and infect one another with new illnesses. As the Cretaceous period went on, more and more land bridges started to appear on the Earth. Because the oceans were drying up and dinosaurs were able to walk across the land bridges, they began to spread new diseases. It is possible that one or more diseases spread through the dinosaur population, causing their extinction.

A third possible cause for the extinction of dinosaurs is the asteroid theory. According to this theory, the extinction was much more sudden and catastrophic. In the 1980s, scientists discovered evidence for the abrupt end to the Age of Dinosaurs. Dr. Luis Alvarez and his colleagues arrived at a revolutionary hypothesis to explain the extinction of dinosaurs. They suggested that about 65 million years ago, the Earth was struck by a huge asteroid. The asteroid was destroyed in the explosion, and billions of tons of dust were thrown up into the air. A thick cloud of dust blocked out sunlight for a long time. Consequently, plants were not able to make food, and they died. The lack of plants killed off many of the plant-eating dinosaurs, which then caused the death of the meat-eating dinosaurs that preyed on them. The darkness caused temperatures to fall below freezing for many months. As a result of this sudden change in climate, the dinosaur populations became smaller and smaller.

It seems that no one theory adequately explains why dinosaurs died out. Perhaps dinosaurs simply could not adjust to the changes that were taking place on the Earth toward the end of the Cretaceous period. Perhaps it was a combination of causes that contributed to the end of the Age of Dinosaurs.

GO ONLINE

Many newspapers and magazines are online. Choose a topic in the news that you are interested in. It can be a local story, a national story, or an international story. Go online to find several articles on the topic. Read the articles, and choose the one that is the most interesting or informative. Print out the article, read it again carefully, and write a one-paragraph summary of it.

YOU BE THE EDITOR

The following paragraph has nine mistakes. Correct the mistakes and copy the revised paragraph on another piece of paper.

In the article "The Growing of Green cars," W. E. Butterworth discusses the new trends in environmentally safe automobiles called "green cars." Automakers are working hardly to produce cars that cause less pollution. They're long-term goal is to make zero-emission vehicles (ZEV) to comply with new state laws. The

Electric cars save energy

author mentions several way that car companies can reach their goal, such as designing cars that burn less fuel, tuning engines so they burn more cleaner fuels, and producing electric cars that do not burn any fuel. However, each one of these solutions has a drawback, and many of them is expensive. Although everyone agree that there are no simple solutions. More and more states are adopting stricter antipollution laws.

ON YOUR OWN

Choose a newspaper or magazine article or find one online on any topic that interests you. Read it carefully, and on a separate piece of paper, write a one-paragraph summary of it. Bring the article and your summary to class to share with your classmates.

Essay Writing: Write a five-paragraph essay that expresses your opinion on a controversial topic

There are many situations where you have to express your opinion. A friend might ask you for advice about a personal matter, or your boss might want your opinion about a project at work. Similarly, many writing tasks involve expressing your opinion. As a writer, you might be asked to give your opinion on a topic in the news or on something you have read, seen, or heard.

© Randy Glasbergen. www.glasbergen.com

2 + 2 = 4

"You're certainly entitled to your opinion."

Opinion papers have an important place in academic writing. You might need to give your opinion on a topic you have discussed or an article you have read. In a literature class, a professor might ask for your reaction to a poem or short story. In a music class, you could be asked to write your reaction to a piece of music.

THE LANGUAGE OF OPINIONS

WRITER'S TIP: Phrases that Introduce Opinions

In my opinion,	I think
To me,	It seems to me
I believe	From my point of view
I strongly believe	I am certain (convinced, sure, positive)
It is my opinion (belief) that	

Expressing Your Opinion about Controversial Issues

A Read the following newspaper article about two convicted murderers who were put to death for crimes they had been convicted of committing many years before.

What Is Justice?

TWO MEN WERE PUT TO DEATH last week in the United States for murders that they had been convicted of committing many years ago. Billy Bailey died in the first hanging in Delaware in fifty years. It was twenty years ago that he murdered an elderly couple after breaking into their home. John Taylor, a child rapist and murderer, was shot by a five-man firing squad in Utah.

Polls show that about 70 percent of U.S. citizens favor capital punishment. Many believe that people who commit horrendous crimes deserve to die brutally in return for the brutality that they inflicted on their victims. Others protest the barbarism of the death penalty, be it by lethal injection, electric chair, firing squad, or hanging. While many people supported the two deaths that took place last week, there were also many protesters.

B In small groups, discuss the article and answer the following questions.

1. What is your opinion about capital punishment? Do you think there are any situations where it is an appropriate method of punishment?

2. Do you think capital punishment helps prevent crime? Why or why not?

3. Do you know of another country that uses capital punishment? Why does that country use it?

C Now read the essay a student wrote that expresses his opinion about the use of capital punishment.

Capital Punishment Is a Crime

Capital punishment, or the death penalty, as it is often called, is one of the oldest forms of punishment. It is also the most controversial. In the United States, the death penalty is used only for the worst crimes, such as premeditated murder. The federal government can seek the death penalty for federal capital crimes (such as treason or the murder of a public official). However, it is up to the individual states to decide whether to allow capital punishment for state offenses. Currently, capital punishment is legal in thirty-six states. In my opinion, that is thirty-six states too many. I believe the death penalty is a barbaric practice that should be abolished not just throughout the United States but also around the world.

First, the death penalty is both immoral and cruel, and it sends the wrong message to society. By legalizing executions, society lowers itself to the same level as the people it condemns to death. There is no doubt that murder—the taking of another person's life—is the most horrible of crimes. However, I think it is fundamentally wrong for the government to punish murderers with murder. Two wrongs don't make a right, and killing someone is wrong, no matter who does it. Capital punishment is also cruel and inhumane. In most states, convicted murderers are put to death by lethal injection. Although this may sound like a relatively humane way to kill someone, there have been cases in which the drugs have not taken effect quickly, causing, most likely, excruciating pain. Causing this kind of suffering on another person, even one whose actions may "justify" it, is clearly an act of cruelty.

Second, I am against the death penalty because it is an ineffective method of punishment. The threat of the death penalty does not make our communities safer. Research shows that the death penalty does not stop people from committing even the most awful crimes. For example, Wisconsin, which has not used the death penalty for 150 years, has a 50 percent lower murder rate than that of states like Texas and Florida, which do use the death penalty.

Finally, and most important, I believe the death penalty should be abolished because it is extremely costly. Studies prove that imprisoning a convicted criminal for life costs much less than keeping a criminal on death row. Keeping a prisoner on death row costs thousands of dollars in extra security. In addition, an average death penalty trial costs a state over a million dollars more than a trial that does not seek the death penalty. The money spent on death penalty cases could be much better spent on crime prevention and on programs that help improve our communities, such as public safety programs, youth programs, drug and alcohol treatment programs, child abuse prevention programs, and assistance programs for crime victims and their families.

Capital punishment is wrong for so many reasons. I can only hope that one day the United States and the other countries around the world that use capital punishment will realize that it is an unacceptable practice. After all, what is the point of having such an awful punishment if it has no positive effect on society?

D **In small groups, discuss the essay and answer the following questions.**

1. What is the student's opinion about the death penalty?

2. What three main reasons does he give to support his opinion?

WRITING ABOUT CONTROVERSIAL ISSUES

Every year, millions of animals are used in medical research, laboratory experiments, and product testing. People around the world are questioning whether this is morally right or wrong. What is your opinion? Do we have the right to use animals for research?

Issue 1

 Prewriting

A **Discuss your opinion about using animals for laboratory experiments with a partner who disagrees with you.**

B **Freewrite about your opinion for ten minutes.**

C Find a partner who agrees with your opinion. Together, brainstorm a list of reasons that support your opinion.

_____   _____

_____   _____

_____   _____

D Use your freewriting and your brainstorming lists as a basis for planning your essay.

Writing

On a separate piece of paper, write the first draft of your essay. Begin with an introduction that includes a thesis statement that asserts your opinion. Organize the supporting paragraphs according to order of importance, beginning or ending with the most important reason. End with a conclusion that summarizes your opinion.

Issue 2

Prewriting

A Choose one of the following topics and freewrite about it for ten minutes on a separate piece of paper.

- your opinion about genetically modified food
- your opinion about women serving in the military
- your opinion about same-sex schools
- your opinion about legal abortions

B Brainstorm a list of reasons, facts, or examples to support your opinion.

_____   _____

_____   _____

_____   _____

C Use your freewriting and your brainstorming list as a basis for planning your essay.

Writing

On a separate piece of paper, write the first draft of your essay. Make sure that you have a clear thesis statement that states your opinion. Discuss one main reason in each supporting paragraph.

Revising and Editing

Exchange drafts with a classmate. Use the checklists on pages 97 and 75. Discuss any suggestions that your partner has for revising and editing. After you revise your essay, hand it in to your teacher.

EXPRESSING YOUR OPINIONS ON EXAM QUESTIONS

Many exams require you to write an essay that expresses your opinion about less controversial issues. You will often have a time limit so you need to work quickly and use your time efficiently. Prewriting and planning are important, so do not skip these steps to save time. Choose one of the following topics and write a five-paragraph essay that expresses your personal opinion.

1. Write your opinion about a song, TV program, or movie. You may choose one that you are familiar with or one that you have just seen or heard for the first time. Use specific reasons and examples to support your opinion.

2. In some countries, teenagers have jobs while they are still students. Is this is a good idea?

3. Some people think the Earth is being harmed by human activity. Others believe that human activity makes the Earth a better place to live. What is your opinion? Use specific reasons and examples to support your opinion.

4. Do you think it is better to enjoy your money when you earn it, or is it better to save your money for the future? Use specific reasons and examples to support your opinion.

5. Do you believe that success in life comes from taking risks or that success results from careful planning? Use specific reasons and examples to support your opinion.

6. Some people believe that governments should spend a lot of money exploring outer space (for example, traveling to Mars, and establishing space stations). Other people disagree and think governments should spend this money for our basic needs at home. Which of these two opinions do you agree with? Use specific reasons and examples to support your opinion.

EXPRESSING YOUR OPINION ABOUT A PIECE OF ART

Painting 1

A **Look at the painting by Jackson Pollock (1912–1956) called *Autumn Rhythm Number 30*. Jackson Pollock was a famous American painter and an important member of the abstract expressionist movement.**

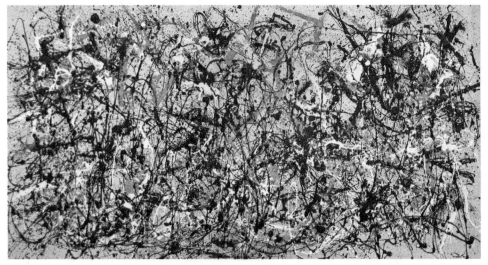

Copyright © Peter Horree / Alamy Stock Photo

B **Think about these questions:**

1. Do you like this kind of art?

2. What is your first reaction to the painting?

C **Read the paragraph that a student wrote expressing her opinion about the painting.**

The first time I saw a Jackson Pollock painting in a museum, I just kept walking because I didn't find it interesting. It seemed too abstract, untraditional, and incomprehensible to me. I wasn't even tempted to stop and read the label. The second time I saw it, I stopped to read the label. I learned that the painting was called *Autumn Rhythm Number 30* and that Pollock put the canvas on the floor and moved around it, pouring and dripping paint from a large brush with big, bold sweeping movements of his arm. He used industrial enamel paint, the kind used on automobiles. The more I looked at the painting, the more I began to appreciate it. I appreciated that he had an unconventional way of painting and that he was freely expressing himself. I began to realize that there is no real subject to his paintings—the physical act of painting is the subject. I realized that I could decide for myself what I see in his paintings but that I must not ascribe my ideas to him. I also loved something that Pollock said. When he was asked about the meaning of his work, he answered with another question, "When you see a flower bed, do you tear your hair out looking for meaning?"

D **Discuss the Jackson Pollock painting and the student's opinion of it with a partner. What is the student's opinion? What is your opinion of the painting now?**

Painting 2

Look at the painting by John Singleton Copley (1738–1815) called *Watson and the Shark*. Then read the information about the artist and the painting.

John Singleton Copley was an important North American painter. He painted huge realistic paintings based on important events of his time. *Watson and the Shark* is one of Copley's most memorable works. It tells the true story of a fourteen-year-old boy, Brook Watson, who was attacked by a shark while he was swimming. Watson was dramatically rescued and later asked Copley to paint a picture of his story.

 ## Prewriting

Discuss the painting with a partner and answer the following questions.

1. What do you see when you look at the painting? Describe the people and their surroundings. You may need to use your dictionary.

2. What is happening in the painting?

3. How does the painting make you feel? Do you like the painting? Why or why not?

Writing

On a separate piece of paper, write a paragraph describing your opinion of *Watson and the Shark*.

Revising and Editing

Exchange drafts with a partner. Use the checklists on pages 97 and 75. Discuss any suggestions that your partner has for revision and editing. Write a revised version of your essay.

Painting 3

Look at the painting by Andrew Wyeth, *Christina's World*. Read the information that follows.

Christina's World, 1948, tempera on panel © Andrew Wyeth

North American painter Andrew Wyeth (1917–2009) is known for his realistic interpretations of people and landscapes, his technical brilliance, and his affection for his subjects. He found inspiration in his everyday surroundings. *Christina's World* is one of Wyeth's best-known paintings.

Prewriting

Discuss your impressions of the painting with a partner and answer the following questions.

1. What do you see when you look at the painting? Describe the woman and her surroundings.

2. What seems to be happening in the painting?

3. What story do you think the artist is trying to tell?

4. What adjectives would you use to describe the painting?

Writing

On a separate piece of paper, write your opinion of *Christina's World*.

Revising and Editing

Exchange drafts with a classmate. Use the checklists on pages 97 and 75. Discuss any suggestions that your partner has for revision and editing. Write a revised version of your essay.

Painting 3 (Follow-up Activity)

Christina's World depicts one of Wyeth's neighbors, a woman named Christina Olson, who was paralyzed. Wyeth's belief that life contains hardship and suffering is reflected by Christina, who stretches awkwardly toward the farmhouse that is beyond her ability to reach.

Look at the painting again, now that you know the story behind it. Answer the following questions.

1. Do you think the painting is about despair and frustration, or do you think the painting is about hope and reaching a goal? Explain your answer.

   _____

   _____

   _____

2. Why do you think the painting is called *Christina's World*?

   _____

   _____

   _____

3. What is your opinion of the painting now that you know the story that Wyeth was trying to tell?

Write a paragraph explaining your new response.

_____

_____

_____

_____

_____

_____

EXPRESSING YOUR OPINION ABOUT A PHOTOGRAPH

 Prewriting

A **Work in a small group. Look at the two photos of hot air balloons.**

B **Answer the following questions.**

1. Describe what is happening in each photograph.

2. Would you like to go up in a hot air balloon? Why or why not?

3. How do the photographs make you feel? Why?

Writing

On a separate piece of paper, write your opinion about one of the photos.

Revising and Editing

Exchange drafts with someone who chose the same photo you did. Compare and contrast your opinions. Then help each other revise and edit using the checklists on pages 97 and 75. Write a revised version of your essay.

RESPONDING TO QUOTATIONS

Many writing assignments involve responding to quotations. You might be asked to explain the meaning of a quotation and then give your opinion of it.

A Read the following quotations from around the world and put a checkmark next to those that you find interesting. In small groups, discuss the quotes that all the members of your group checked.

_____ 1. *Anyone who looks for a perfect friend will remain without friends.* (Turkish proverb)

_____ 2. *Happiness sneaks in through a door you didn't know you left open.* (John Barrymore)

_____ 3. *Winning is neither everything nor the only thing; it is one of many things.* (Joan Benoit Samuelson)

_____ 4. *A human life is like a letter of the alphabet. It can be meaningless. Or it can be part of a great meaning.* (Anonymous)

_____ 5. *Anyone who has never made a mistake has never tried anything new.* (Albert Einstein)

_____ 6. *A pessimist sees the difficulty in every opportunity; an optimist sees the opportunity in every difficulty.* (Winston Churchill)

_____ 7. *Keep your eyes on the stars and your feet on the ground.* (Theodore Roosevelt)

_____ 8. *The man who removes mountains begins by carrying away small stones.* (Chinese proverb)

_____ 9. *Without struggle there can be no progress.* (Frederick Douglass)

_____ 10. *If you reject the food, ignore the customs, fear the religion and avoid the people, you might better stay home.* (James Michener)

_____ 11. *A journey of a thousand miles starts with a single step.* (Lao Tzu)

_____ 12. *I hear and I forget. I see and I remember. I do and I understand.* (Confucius)

_____ 13. *The only way to have a friend is to be a friend.* (Ralph Waldo Emerson)

_____ 14. *I find that the harder I work, the more luck I seem to have.* (Thomas Jefferson)

_____ 15. *Those who cannot feel the littleness of great things in themselves are apt to overlook the greatness of little things in others.* (Kakuzo Okakura)

_____ 16. *You can tell whether a man is clever by his answers. You can tell whether a man is wise by his questions.* (Naguib, Mahfouz)

_____ 17. *Give a man a fish and you feed him for a day. Teach a man to fish and you feed him for a lifetime.* (Chinese proverb)

_____ 18. *Statistically 100 percent of the shots you don't take don't go in.* (Wayne Gretsky)

_____ 19. *The best way to cheer yourself up is to try to cheer somebody else up.* (Mark Twain)

_____ 20. *This we know—the Earth does not belong to man—man belongs to the Earth. This we know. All things are connected like the blood which unites one family. All things are connected. Whatever befalls the Earth—befalls the sons of the Earth. Man did not weave the web of life—he is merely a strand in it. Whatever he does to the web, he does to himself.* (Chief Seattle)

(B) **Choose one of the quotes you discussed with your group and write a one-paragraph response to it on another piece of paper. Be sure to include the quote at the beginning of your paragraph. Explain why you chose that quote and how it has meaning for you.**

(C) **Read your reactions to the other members of your group for their feedback. Then revise, edit, and rewrite your response on a separate piece of paper before handing it in.**

EXPRESSING YOUR OPINION THROUGH POETRY

Poem 1

Read the information about Robert Frost and his poem "The Road Not Taken."
Robert Frost (1874–1963) is one of the most important North American poets of the twentieth century. "The Road Not Taken" tells the story of an important choice the author made in his life.

The Road Not Taken

I. Two roads diverged in a yellow wood,[1]
And sorry I could not travel both
And be one traveler, long I stood
And looked down one as far as I could
To where it bent in the undergrowth;[2]

II. Then took the other, as just as fair,[3]
And having perhaps the better claim,
Because it was grassy and wanted wear;[4]
Though as for that the passing there
Had worn them really about the same,

III. And both that morning equally lay
In leaves no step had trodden black.[5]
Oh, I kept the first for another day!
Yet knowing how way leads on to way,[6]
I doubted if I should ever come back.

IV. I shall be telling this with a sigh
Somewhere ages and ages hence:[7]
Two roads diverged in a wood, and I—
I took the one less traveled by,
And that has made all the difference.

—*Robert Frost*

[1] One road divided into two roads in a forest.
[2] To the place where it turned under the low bushes
[3] I took the other road, which was just as nice.
[4] Because it was slightly overgrown and less used
[5] No one had walked on either road yet that day.
[6] I knew how one road often leads to another road.
[7] In some time in the future

Prewriting

The four stanzas (groups of lines) of the poem each tell a part of the story. Read each stanza again and think about what it means. Then look at the following summaries. Each summary refers to one of the stanzas in the poem. Match each summary with the stanza it refers to.

1. He decided to take the road that looked like it had not been used as much.

   Stanza: _____

2. Sometime in the future, he will remember this day when he had to make a choice and be glad that he took the road that was less traveled.

   Stanza: _____

3. A man was walking in the woods, and he came to a place where the single road divided into two separate roads. He was sorry that he could not take both roads.

   Stanza: _____

4. Although he chose the second road, he hoped that he would be able to return some day to take the first one. But he doubted that he ever would.

   Stanza: _____

Writing

Robert Frost's poem is based on a choice he had to make. Think about an important choice that you have made. On a separate piece of paper, describe the situation and the effect your choice has had on your life.

Revising and Editing

Exchange drafts with a classmate. Use the checklists on pages 97 and 75. Discuss any suggestions that your partner has for revision and editing. Write a revised version of your essay to hand in.

Poem 2

Read the information about Emily Dickinson and her poem "Hope Is the Thing with Feathers."

Emily Dickinson (1830–1886) is another of North America's gifted poets. "Hope Is the Thing with Feathers" is one of Dickinson's most famous poems. In this poem, she uses the metaphor of a bird to describe her feelings about hope.

Hope Is the Thing with Feathers

Hope is the thing with feathers
That perches[1] in the soul,
And sings the tune without the words,
And never stops at all.

And sweetest in the Gale[2] is heard;
And sore must be the storm
That could abash[3] the little Bird
That kept so many warm.

I've heard it in the chillest land,
And on the strangest Sea;
Yet, never, in Extremity,[4]
It asked a crumb[5] of Me.

—Emily Dickinson

[1] Sits
[2] Strong wind
[3] Upset
[4] An extreme situation
[5] A small piece of food

 Prewriting

Discuss your opinion of the poem with a partner.

Metaphor Activity

A metaphor is a phrase that describes something by comparing it to something else without the words *like* or *as*. Reread the first two lines of Emily Dickinson's poem. Using these lines as a model, create your own metaphors for each of the following words.

1. Happiness is a/an _____ *flower* _____ with _____ *buds* _____

   that *blossom in my heart* _____.

2. Jealousy is a/an _____ with _____

   that _____.

3. Beauty is a/an _____ with _____

   that _____.

4. Hate is a/an _____ with _____

   that _____.

5. Love is a/an _____ with _____

   that _____.

6. Wisdom is a/an _____ with _____

   that _____.

7. Fear is a/an _____ with _____

   that _____.

 ## Writing

Emily Dickinson describes hope as a thing with feathers. How would you describe hope? Write a paragraph about one of the following topics on a separate piece of paper:

1. A time in your life when hope was very important

2. Your hopes for the future

3. Your own description of hope

 ## Revising and Editing

Exchange drafts with a classmate. Use the checklists on pages 97 and 75. Discuss any suggestions that your partner has for revising and editing. Write a revised version of your essay to hand in.

WRITING YOUR OWN POEM: HAIKU

Haiku is a very old form of poetry from Japan. Haiku poems are usually about nature. The form of a haiku is always the same. It contains three lines:

- The first line has five syllables.
- The second line has seven syllables.
- The third line has five syllables.

Matsuo Basho (1644–1694) was a well-known haiku master. This is a translation of one of his most famous haikus.

At the ancient pond
a frog plunges right into
the sound of water

   —*Matsuo Basho*

Here are some examples of haikus that students have written.

Look up in the sky
See the blue birds flying high
Over the ocean

    —Vasakorn Bhadranavik

Noisy rain has stopped
White snow covers everything
Silent night has come

    —Kazu Karasawa

The birds of passage
Are taking a winter's rest
Ready to go south

    —Fumihiko Suita

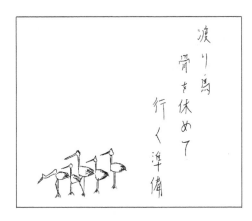

A **Choose a season and a scene from nature that you would like to write about. Think about the picture that you want to create in your readers' minds. Then follow the steps to write your own haiku.**

Season: _____

Scene from nature: _____

_____

B **Decide what your first line will be. Work on the words until you have exactly five syllables. Write it on the first of the following three lines.**

C Write your second line. Remember that it must contain seven syllables.

D Write your third line. Make sure it contains five syllables.

_____

_____

_____

E Exchange your haiku with a partner. Make sure the syllable count is correct for each line. Discuss your haikus.

GO ONLINE

1. The Internet has many lists of famous sayings. A saying is a short, clever expression that often contains advice or expresses a truth. Go online and find some of these lists. Write down five sayings you find interesting because you agree or disagree with them. Then, share your list with your classmates. Choose one and write a paragraph explaining your own opinion of the saying.

2. Find pictures of several pieces of art or examples of architecture on the Internet. Choose one and write your reaction to it.

3. Go to the website of your favorite newspaper. Read two opinion letters or editorials about the same topic. Write a paragraph explaining which opinion you agree with.

YOU BE THE EDITOR

The following email has seven mistakes. Find the mistakes and correct them.

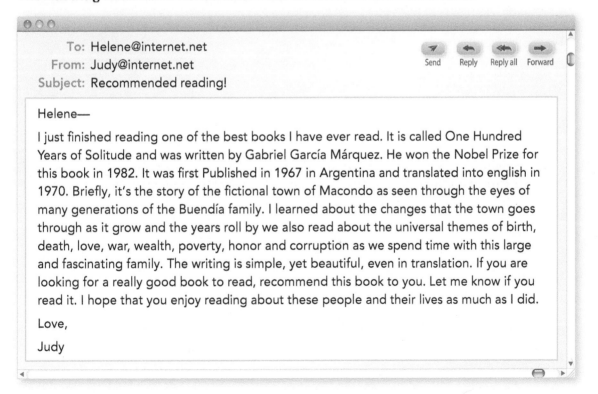

To: Helene@internet.net
From: Judy@internet.net
Subject: Recommended reading!

Helene—

I just finished reading one of the best books I have ever read. It is called One Hundred Years of Solitude and was written by Gabriel García Márquez. He won the Nobel Prize for this book in 1982. It was first Published in 1967 in Argentina and translated into english in 1970. Briefly, it's the story of the fictional town of Macondo as seen through the eyes of many generations of the Buendía family. I learned about the changes that the town goes through as it grow and the years roll by we also read about the universal themes of birth, death, love, war, wealth, poverty, honor and corruption as we spend time with this large and fascinating family. The writing is simple, yet beautiful, even in translation. If you are looking for a really good book to read, recommend this book to you. Let me know if you read it. I hope that you enjoy reading about these people and their lives as much as I did.

Love,

Judy

ON YOUR OWN

You are an employee at ZipCo and have just received this memo. Write an email or a letter to your parents or a close friend that expresses your opinion about this news.

MEMO

TO: All ZipCo Employees
FROM: Jim Philips
RE: Merger with Logicom
DATE: June 30, 2016

As most of you know, we have been talking for several months now with the people at Logicom about merging our two companies. We are pleased to announce that the details have been worked out, and we will be combining our companies. The official merger date is set for October 15. We are confident that we can look forward to a long and successful alliance with Logicom since our products complement each other so well. This merger should lead to greater success in the marketplace than either company could achieve on its own.

This memo is also to confirm that as per Logicom's insistence, we will be moving our offices and people to Montreal. We know that this will be difficult and disruptive for some of you, but we sincerely believe that it is in the best interest of the company. We hope that each and every one of you will join us in this exciting opportunity. Further details regarding the merger and the move will be sent to you shortly.

Essay Writing: Write an undergraduate or graduate application essay

If you are planning to apply to undergraduate or graduate school in the United States, you will probably have to write a personal essay as part of the application process. Some schools will give you very structured questions while others will give you more open-ended questions. In this chapter, you will practice writing answers to typical essay questions for applications.

PLANNING YOUR APPLICATION ESSAY

Whether you are applying to undergraduate or graduate school, there are several principles that you should pay attention to in writing your essay. Even if you are not planning to attend a university in the United States, you will improve your writing skills by practicing this kind of essay.

WHAT IF I CAN'T AFFORD COLLEGE?
WHAT IF THERE'S A WAR?
WHAT IF I CAN'T FIND A JOB?
WHAT IF I END UP IN A CARTOON?
WHAT IF THE CARTOON ISN'T FUNNY?

GLASBERGEN
© Randy Glasbergen / glasbergen.com

Tips for Writing a College Application Essay

1. **Take the essay part of the application very seriously.** To some schools, the essay is the most important part of your application. Admissions officers at more than one school have said that the essay can make or break a candidate's chances for admission.

2. **Be honest. Be yourself. Be sincere.** The admissions committees want to know who you are as a person. Do not misrepresent yourself.

3. **Write about something that is important to you.** Even if you are given a specific subject to write about, you will have to choose your angle. Let your enthusiasm for the subject show. Your interest in the subject is a very important—sometimes the most important—element in an essay.

4. **Make your application as interesting and lively as you can.** Admissions officers read hundreds, maybe thousands, of essays. You want yours to stand out.

5. **Do not try to write the application essay in a hurry or at the last minute.** You need to give yourself time to think about the question and do some prewriting and planning before you actually write the essay.

6. **Keep your audience and your purpose in mind as you plan and write your essay.**

7. **Pay attention to the principles of good writing that you have studied in this book.** Make sure you have a main idea, support, and clear organization. Include specific details so that your essay is uniquely about you. Do not write an essay that is so general that it could have been written by any number of other people. Add details to bring your essay to life.

8. **Follow the rules you have learned in this book for writing a good introduction, body, and conclusion.**

9. **Your essay must be as perfect as you can make it.** This means no grammatical, spelling, punctuation, or capitalization mistakes. Have several people—teachers, relatives, and/or friends—read it carefully for you. Remember that neatness counts.

10. **Make a copy of your essay before you mail it.** This will avoid problems if your application gets lost in the mail or in the admissions office. To be safe, send it registered mail with a return receipt requested.

UNDERGRADUATE ESSAYS

The application essay is very important to admissions committees. They use it to get to know the individual behind the test scores and the grade point average. You should think of your essay as a chance to show yourself off to your best advantage. Try to tell them a little more about yourself than they would know by reading the rest of your application. Admissions committees also use the essay to determine how well you write because good writing skills are important for success in college. In short, your essay is your special opportunity to prove that you are an interesting person and that you can write well.

Analyzing an Undergraduate Essay

Here is a sample essay that a student wrote on his application form.

Read the essay and then answer the questions.

APPLICATION FORM

In reading your application, we want to get to know you as well as we can. We ask that you use this opportunity to tell us something more about yourself that would help us get a sense of who you are, how you think, and what issues and ideas interest you the most.

Scuba diving has never been easy for me. When I was in fifth grade, the father of one of my classmates died in a scuba diving accident. His death, along with the scenes I had watched in James Bond movies of men left to drown hundreds of feet under water with severed air tubes, did not give me the impression that scuba diving was a safe sport. However, in eighth grade, my father asked me if I would take scuba diving classes with him. Although I was reluctant, the important consideration was that he would be there to support me and that we would do it together. It seemed that as I grew older, we spent less time together. I wanted this opportunity to be with him.

After hours of pool work and classes, I was ready to go for my certification. My first problem was getting to the dive site. I have a slight fear of boats, which probably stems from my first boat ride, during which I developed a major case of seasickness. This was a small obstacle compared to what was about to come. I spent the first fifteen minutes of the dive standing on the rocking deck of the dive boat, staring at the rough ocean, weak with fear. I was only able to dive into the water after a good pep talk from both my father and my dive master. I repeated the word "relax" to myself over and over and plunged in.

Even now, after five years of scuba diving, I still feel a little uneasy before submerging. However, once I have taken a deep breath and broken the surface of the water, curiosity and astonishment at the variety on the ocean floor calm my apprehensions. No sounds or disturbances break the perfect tranquility. Enormous purple fans wave in the current, and orange and red sponges jut out of the coral like poppies in a meadow. When I am underwater, I can hover above the colorful, craggy coral, flying like Superman, watching schools of fish dart around in search of food, oblivious to my presence. Underwater, I am able to leave behind my worries and observe the peaceful beauty of nature.

The experience does not end with my surfacing but continues with the stories my father, the other divers, and I tell afterward. There is a high level of camaraderie among all divers. We sit around like old pirates in a dank tavern, laughing as we talk about the stingrays who search for food in our hair (an experience that was once described as "like being mugged by E.T.") or about the dive master who found a bicycle down by one of the wrecks and started to ride it around. My fellow divers do not know that I have not yet left behind my fears of diving because, once I submerge, I inhabit a different world with them.

Like learning to scuba dive, learning to read was also not easy for me. Most early-reading programs rely heavily on the teaching of phonetics. However, I have a learning disability that makes understanding sound/symbol relationships difficult. This made learning to read through the use of phonetics impossible. I was lucky, though, because I was accepted into Fenn School's Intensive Language Program. For two years (fourth and fifth grades), six other boys and I worked together, learning how to compensate for our learning differences. In this class, I developed a trait that I am very proud of: the ability to work hard—not only in my studies, but in everything I do.

By continuing even when the waters were rough, and drawing on the support of my parents and teachers, I learned to read and found an amazing world opened to me. Just as my fellow divers do not know that I am anxious about scuba diving, most of my classmates do not know that I have a learning disability. They just think that I am a diligent worker, but I know that, as with scuba diving, there is a lot more to the story.

1. What two experiences did the student write about? How are they related? What was his purpose in talking about scuba diving?

_____

_____

_____

2. What did you learn about this student? What adjectives would you use to describe him?

_____

_____

_____

3. What does the essay reveal about the student's relationship with his father?

_____

_____

_____

4. What did you learn about the student's values?

_____

_____

_____

Sample Essay Questions

The most common application essay is the one that asks you for autobiographical information. Some schools ask for it directly with questions such as, "Tell us a little about yourself" or "Give the admissions committee information about yourself that is not included elsewhere on the application." Other schools ask the question indirectly with such questions as, "What person has influenced you the most in life?"

Here are some typical essay topics often used by colleges and universities in the United States. In small groups, discuss the topics and make notes about how to answer each one.

1. Evaluate a significant experience or achievement that has special meaning to you.

2. Discuss some issue of personal, local, or national concern and its importance to you.

3. Indicate a person who has had a significant influence on you and describe that influence.

4. What one word best describes you and why?

5. If you could change any event in history, what would you change and why?

6. Describe the most difficult thing that you have ever done.

7. What book has affected you most and why?

8. Describe a change that you have gone through and how it may affect your future.

WRITING AN UNDERGRADUATE APPLICATION ESSAY

Prewriting

A Choose three of the essay topics above and, on a separate piece of paper, freewrite about each one for ten minutes.

B Reread your three freewriting samples and choose one of them to develop into an essay. Using the ideas you generated in your prewriting, prepare an outline of the essay.

Writing

On a separate piece of paper, write the first draft of your essay. Be sure to start with an interesting introduction that will make the admissions committee excited about reading your essay. You should choose a method of organization for your supporting paragraphs, such as time order or order of importance, that best suits your topic. Include specific details and examples that will help the committee get to know you. Finally, make your conclusion one that the readers will remember.

Revising and Editing

A Wait at least one day and then revise your essay using the checklist on page 97. Write a revised version of your essay.

B Use the checklist on page 75 to edit your essay. Correct all the grammar, punctuation, capitalization, and spelling errors. Give your essay to your teacher and someone else to read for any final comments before you rewrite it.

WRITER'S TIP: Get Second Opinions

Ask other people to read your essay before you submit it. Then, you can use their feedback to improve your essay.

GRADUATE SCHOOL ESSAYS

The biggest difference between essays for undergraduate and graduate school is the subject matter. A graduate school essay focuses on career goals and is generally referred to as a personal statement. The tips for writing application essays that you read on page 206 are useful for both types of essays.

Analyzing a Graduate School Personal Statement

Here is an example of a successful graduate school personal statement essay. This student wants to study civil engineering at the University of Michigan.

Read the essay and then answer the questions.

PERSONAL STATEMENT

Your personal statement should be a concise, well-written essay about your background, your career goals, and how Michigan's graduate program will help you meet your career and educational objectives.

My lifelong passion for structures and construction was sparked in 1978 when I got my first LEGO set. I would spend hours imagining and drawing buildings and bridges and trying to make them out of LEGO pieces. My father is a civil engineer, and one of my greatest joys was accompanying him to oversee the progress at his construction sites. Nothing was more intriguing to me then than watching a structure transform from a sketch on an engineer's pad to a building in our community. I can still remember the sense of pride I felt upon the completion of the dam my father had engineered. Ever since I was a child, my dream has been to become a civil engineer and join my father in his company. Over the years, my dream has not changed, but the path to my goal has become more complicated. As I watched Turkey go through a series of political and economic changes, I felt the great effect it had on companies like my father's. I came to realize that in order to be a successful civil engineer, I would need to acquire a diversity of skills.

When I was in high school, the Turkish economy was tightly held in the hands of the government. Almost all major industries were dominated by government monopolies, leaving little room for the private sector to flourish. Then, seemingly overnight, Turkey went from an economy based on small family businesses and government-held industries to a competitive market modeled on the Western style. The privatization of Turkish industries in the late 1980s and a concurrent influx of foreign investments led to the birth of big corporations in all industries, including construction. However, the transition has not always been a smooth one. Turkey lacked a solid core of educated business professionals capable of dealing with the rapid economic growth that involved newly defined business relations at corporate levels. There was only a handful of Turkish businesspeople skilled at negotiating with managers of foreign companies.

Realizing this need, I decided that the first step of my educational plan should be to study business and finance at a university in the United States. This would provide me with the solid foundation of knowledge and skills that I would need in my construction management career. When I left home to come to the United States, Turkey was on the brink of a new era. During the five years that I have been here completing my undergraduate education, Turkey has undergone tremendous changes in all spheres: political, social, economic, and technological.

Old systems and traditional models were replaced with contemporary ones as Western influences became more dominant.

During the past five years, I have become fluent in English while earning a bachelor of science degree in finance, with a minor in economics. I am currently completing a second bachelor's degree in mathematics. Now, I will further my education by pursuing graduate studies in civil engineering. Turkey's recent economic boom has brought an unprecedented wave of unmanaged construction in urban areas, revealing a need for highly trained engineers with managerial skills. The Construction Engineering and Management program at the University of Michigan will expand upon my present management knowledge and train me in the engineering skills necessary to plan, coordinate, and influence the diverse range of specialists involved in the construction industry. I feel that my background in economics and finance, coupled with my strong quantitative skills, makes me an excellent candidate for graduate studies in this field.

Michigan's Construction Engineering and Management program will prepare me for a responsible management position in the construction industry. At Michigan, I hope to be involved in research that investigates the applications of artificial intelligence techniques as well as computer applications in the construction industry. I would also like to research strategies for innovation in construction, especially as they relate to a developing country. Finally, I am interested in how the planning, design, and implementation of engineering projects are integrated into a coherent, well-functioning system. I hope to improve my understanding of the whole system by examining how the subsystems and various components fit together.

Since one of my goals is to improve the operation and management of Turkey's current inefficient infrastructure, I would like to study ways of improving efficiency in the use of labor and natural resources. This will involve rebuilding, restoring, and upgrading a rapidly deteriorating infrastructure as well as creating new physical structures that reflect the application of modern technology. Turkey desperately needs new airports, harbors, highways, public transportation systems, and industrial plants to facilitate its rapid economic growth. The engineering problems Turkey faces require professionals who are able to bring together ideas from technology, science, and systems and operations management.

By earning an M.S. degree in construction engineering and management, I will return to Turkey equipped with the most sophisticated knowledge in my field. I hope not only to learn practical information that I can apply to the situation in Turkey, but also to acquire the theoretical basis and research skills necessary to identify structural, managerial, and economic problems and formulate strategies for solutions. My ultimate goal is to be a professional with the ability to implement my vision for the future of Turkey.

1. What did this essay tell you about the student's background?

_____

_____

2. Why do you think the student mentioned playing with LEGO pieces in the introduction?

_____

_____

3. Why is the student interested in studying engineering?

_____

_____

4. What experiences led him to this interest?

_____

_____

5. How has he prepared himself for graduate school?

_____

_____

6. What qualities do you detect about this student that will make him successful in graduate school?

_____

_____

WRITING A PERSONAL STATEMENT ESSAY

Practice writing a personal statement essay. Respond to the following sample writing prompt:

Discuss your educational background, work experience, and career objectives. Be as specific as you can about the area in which you plan to study.

_____

_____

_____

_____

_____

_____

_____

_____

Prewriting

A Choose one of the prewriting techniques that you are comfortable with. Use this space to generate ideas.

_____

_____

_____

_____

_____

_____

_____

_____

_____

_____

_____

_____

B Organize your prewriting by making an informal outline on a separate piece of paper.

Writing

On a separate piece of paper, write the first draft of your essay. Use your outline as a guide.

Revising and Editing

A Wait at least one day and then revise your essay using the checklist on page 97. Write or type a revised version of your essay.

B Use the checklist on page 75 to edit your essay. Correct all the grammar, punctuation, capitalization, and spelling errors. Give your essay to your teacher and someone else to read for any final comments before you rewrite it.

FILLING OUT A COLLEGE APPLICATION

Many colleges and universities in the United States use the same application form. It is called the Common Application or Common App for short. It has an online version which is very popular although some schools put their own application online. Go online and find an online college application, or the Common App, and fill it out for practice. Remember not to press "Send"!

Most applications also include several short-answer questions. Do not be deceived by these questions. They are just as important as the longer essay questions, and the same principles apply.

YOU BE THE EDITOR

This paragraph has six mistakes. Correct the mistakes and copy the revised paragraph on another piece of paper.

I am interested in mathematic and science, but at this point I have not yet identified a specific area to major in. I am also interest in learning more about the field of engineering. At Blake University I can to explore all of these areas, before I decide upon a major. Blake even offer the opportunity to combine them into an interdisciplinary major. finally, although I do not intend to major in art, I have a strong interest in art and find the possible of taking courses at Blake's School of Design attractive.

Appendix
Answer Key

Chapter 1
Chapter Highlights, p. 24

1. subject, purpose, audience
2. prewriting, writing, revising and editing
3. brainstorming, clustering, freewriting, keeping a journal
4. making a simple outline

Chapter 2
Chapter Highlights, p. 50

1. a single topic
2. topic sentence
3. controls
4. support the topic sentence
5. providing the specific reasons, details, and /or examples
6. topic
7. focus
8. specific details
9. single focus
10. logical order
11. relate
12. time order
13. spatial order
14. order of importance
15. transitions (signal words or phrases)

CHAPTER 3
You Be the Editor, p. 77

> *N Y C*

There are a lot of interesting things to see and do in ~~new york city~~. It is home to more than 150

> *There*

world-class museums. ~~Their~~ are art museums, science museums, photography museums, natural

> *its*

history museums, and even a museum of seaport history. New York is known for ~~their~~ rich variety of

theater, music, and dance. From the bright lights of Broadway and the respected stages at Lincoln

Center and Carnegie Hall to the high kicks of the Rockettes at Radio City Music Hall and incredible jazz

> *for*

at intimate clubs, there is something for everyone. Many people go to New York. ~~For~~ the wonderful

restaurants. There are thousands of restaurants to please every palate and wallet. If you are looking

> *, you*

for a place to shop. ~~You~~ will find everything you can imagine. With more than 10,000 shops filled with

> *As*

brand names and bargains from around the world, NYC are a shopper's paradise. ~~as~~ for me,

people-watching is my favorite New York pastime.

CHAPTER 3
Chapter Highlights, p. 77–78

1. revising
2. editing
3. improve
4. add new ideas
5. eliminate irrelevant sentences
6. rearrange ideas
7. topic sentence
8. relate
9. delete
10. logical order
11. transitions
12. details
13. facts
14. examples
15. reasons
16. grammar
17. punctuation
18. spelling

CHAPTER 4
Chapter Highlights, p. 99

1. introduction, body, conclusion; introduction (captures reader's interest, provides background information, and states the main idea), body (develops main points about the subject with specific details, facts, and examples), conclusion (restates the thesis, summarizes the main ideas, and leaves the reader with something to think about)

2. move from general to specific, use an anecdote, use a quotation, ask a question, present facts and statistics

3. restate main points, ask a question, suggest a solution or make a recommendation or prediction

CHAPTER 5
You Be the Editor, p. 114

If you like to eat or bake delicious cookies, you will love this recipe. Soften ½ pound of butter and mix it together with 2 cups off sugar. Stir in 3 beaten egg*s* and 5 tablespoons of lemon juice. Then add 4 cups of flour,^ 1 teaspoon of baking powder, and 2 ½ teaspoons of nutmeg. As soon as the mixture is thoroughly combined, form the dough into a large ball and refrigerat*e* ~~refrigerator~~ it for at least 1 hour. When *you're* ~~your~~ ready to bake the cookies, divide the ball of dough in half. Roll the dough out so that *it* ^ is ½ inch thick. It will be easier if you use a rolling pin. Cut the cookies into shapes, using the open end of a glass or cookie cutters if you have them. Put the cookies on greased cookie sheets and bake them at 375° for 6 minutes. To make them sweeter and more festive, frost them with colored frosting. Don't eat t*o*o^ many!

CHAPTER 6
You Be the Editor, p. 128

Consumer products are usually divided into three groups: convenience, shopping, and specialty products. Each group is based on the way people buys products. Convenience products are products that a consumer needs but that he or she is not willing to spend very much time or effort shopping for. Convenience products *are* usually inexpensive, frequently purchased items. Some common examples are bread, newspapers, soda, and gasoline. Buyers spend *little* ~~few~~ time planning the purchase of a convenience product. *They also* ~~Also~~ do not compare brands or sellers. The second group, shopping products, are those products that customers feel are worth the time and effort to compare with competing products. Furniture, refrigerators, cars, and televisions are examples of shopping products. Because these products are expected to last a long time, *they* ~~They~~ are purchased less frequently than convenience products. The last group consists of specialty products. Specialty products are consumer products that the customer really wants and makes a special effort to find and ~~buying~~. Buyers actually plan the purchase of a specialty product. They know what they want and will not accept a substitute. A high-tech camera, a pair of skis, and a haircut by a certain stylist are examples of specialty products. In searching for specialty products, *buyers* ~~Buyers~~ do not compare alternatives.

CHAPTER 7
You Be the Editor, p. 147

The Great Depression of the 1930s affected the United States for generations. The collapse of the stock market began on October 24, 1929, when 13 million shares of stock were sold. On October 29, known as Black Tuesday, 16 million shares were sold. The value of most shares fell sharply, resulting in financial ruin for many and widespread panic. Although there have been other financial panics, *none* ~~None~~ had such a devastating effect as the Great Depression. By 1932, the industrial output of the US had been cut in half. About 15 million people *were* ~~was~~ out of work; and salaries dropped almost 50%. In addition, hundreds of banks *failed* ~~will fail~~. Prices for agricultural products dropped drastically. Over 90,000 businesses failed complete.^ly Statistics, however, cannot tell the story of the hardships the masses of

people suffered. For nearly every unemployed ~~people~~ person, there were dependents who needed food

and housing. People in the United States had never known such poverty and hunger before. Former

millionaires stood on street corners selling apples for 5 cents. Thousands ~~lose~~ lost their homes,^,b Because

they could not pay ~~there~~ their mortgages. Some people moved in with relatives. Others built shelters from

tin cans and cardboard. Homeless people slept outside under newspapers. Thousands waited in lines

in every city, hoping for something to eat. Unfortunately, many died of malnutrition. In 1931, more

than 20,000 people committed suicide.

CHAPTER 8
You Be the Editor, p. 161

Now that I am pregnant with our first child, my husband and I will have to find a bigger place

to live. Our little apartment in the city is too small for three people. We^are trying to decide whether we

should get a bigg~~est~^er apartment in the city or move to the suburbs. We have four main consideration^s:

expense, space, convenience, and schools. In general,^it is probably ~~expensiver~~ more expensive to live in the city.

On the other hand, we would have to buy a car if we moved to the suburbs^. We we would also have

to buy a lawnmower and a snow blower or hire someone^to care for the lawn and driveway. In terms

of space, we could definitely have a bigger house and much more land if we lived in the suburbs.

However, we wonder if it would be worth it, since we would lose so many conveniences. Stores

would be farther away, and so would friends, neighbors, movie theaters, museums, and restaurants.

The ~~most~~ biggest inconvenience would be that we would both have to commute to work every day

instead of walking or taking the bus. The schools are probably better in the suburbs, but for our child,

who isn't even born yet, school is several years away. In looking at our priorities, it becomes clear

that we should continue to live in the city for now and then reevaluate our decision as the baby gets

closer to school age.

CHAPTER 9
You Be the Editor, p. 174

If you are like most people, you average one to three colds per year. Even if you do not have a cold right now, The chances are three in four that within the next year, at least one cold virus will find you. Then you'll spend a week or so suffering from the miseries of the common cold: fatigue, sore throat, laryngitis, sneezing, stuffy or runny nose, and coughing. According to researchers, colds are the most common medical reason for missing school and work. Once you catch a cold, what can you do? There is no known cure yet for a cold. There are, however, several thing you can do to suppress the symptom so that you feel better while the virus runs its course. For example, make sure that you get plenty of sleep and drink lots of liquids. You may find commercially available cold remedies such as decongestants, cough suppressants, and expectorants helpful, but keep in mind that these products can cause side effects. Many people prefer home remedies such as chicken soup, garlic, and ginger tea. In treating a cold, remember the wisdom of the ages, "if you treat a cold, it will be gone in a week; if you don't treat it, will be gone in seven days."

Source: *Jane Brody's Cold and Flu Fighter*

CHAPTER 10
You Be the Editor, p. 187

In the article "The Growing of Green cars," W. E. Butterworth discusses the new trends in environmentally safe automobiles called "green cars." Automakers are working hardly to produce cars that cause less pollution. They're long-term goal is to make zero-emission vehicles (ZEV) to comply with new state laws. The author mentions several way that car companies can reach their goal, such as designing cars that burn less fuel, tuning engines so they burn more cleaner fuels, and producing electric cars that do not burn any fuel. However, each one of these solutions has a drawback, and many of them is expensive. Although everyone agree that there are no simple solutions, More and more states are adopting stricter antipollution laws.

CHAPTER 11
You Be the Editor, p. 203

Helene—

    I just finished reading one of the best books I have ever read. It is called *One Hundred Years of Solitude* and was written by Gabriel García Márquez. He won the Nobel Prize for this book in 1982. It was first ~~p~~Published in 1967 in Argentina and translated into ~~e~~English in 1970. Briefly, it's the story of the fictional town of Macondo as seen through the eyes of many generations of the Buendiá family. I learned about the changes that the town goes through as it grow*s* and the years roll by*,* we also read about the universal themes of birth, death, love, war, wealth, poverty, honor*,* and corruption as we spend time with this large and fascinating family. The writing is simple, yet beautiful, even in translation. If you are looking for a really good book to read, *I* recommend this book to you. Let me know if you read it. I hope that you enjoy reading about these people and their lives as much as I did.

Love,
Judy

CHAPTER 12
You Be the Editor, p. 214

    I am interested in mathematic*s* and science, but at this point I have not yet identified a specific area to major in. I am also interest*ed* in learning more about the field of engineering. At Blake University I can ~~to~~ explore all of these areas, before I decide upon a major. Blake even offer*s* the opportunity to combine them into an interdisciplinary major. ~~f~~Finally, although I do not intend to major in art, I have a strong interest in art and find the ~~possible~~ *possibility* of taking courses at Blake's School of Design attractive.

Text Credits

Text credits: p. 9. From Dave Barry's *Only Travel Guide You'll Ever Need,* by Dave Barry, Fawcett Columbine Books, New York, 1991, pp. 19, 20. **29.** Source: *Dos and Taboos around the World,* edited by Roger Axtell, John Wiley and Sons, Inc., New York 1993. **29.** Source: *Encarta* 1994, "Pets." Microsoft. **39.** Source: *Car and Travel,* "Seven Stress-Busters for Air Travelers," by Anne Kelleher, Nov.–Dec. 1995, pp. 8–9. **41.** From Carol Varley and Lisa Miles, *The USBORNE Geography Encyclopedia,* E.D.C. Publishers, Tulsa, Oklahoma, p. 24. **72.** From "Pet Therapy," Sy Montgomery, *Cobblestone,* June 1985, p. 21. **76.** From "Sleeping Well," Nick Gallo, Your Health and Fitness, p. 7. **93.** "How to Make an Object Disappear" by Daniel Blanchard. Reprinted by permission. **116.** "Where Are the Bees?" by Daniel Blanchard. Reprinted by permission. **130.** Sources: "The 'Jim' Twins" by Betty Springer, *Good Housekeeping,* February 1980, pp. 123, 206, 208, **210.** "Double Mystery" by Lawrence Wright, *New Yorker,* August 7, 1995, pp. 49–50. **141.** "Energy Sources: A Dilemma for the 21st century" by Alan Bronstein. Reprinted with permission. **145.** "Solving the World's Food Shortage Crisis" by Daniel Blanchard. Reprinted by permission. **150.** Source: *Jane Brody's Cold and Flu Fighter,* Jane Brody, W. W. Norton Company, New York, 1995. **156.** Amy Barth "The New Theory about Why Animals Sleep: To Maintain the Immune System" March 22, 2009, from Discover Magazine. **157.** "A Chimp Off the Old Block," Curtis Rist, *Discover* magazine, January 2002. Reprinted with permission. **159.** "Politics As Usual" by Diana Childress. From *Cobblestone* April 1995 issue: *Franklin D. Roosevelt,* © 1995, Cobblestone Publishing, Inc., 30 Grove Street, Suite C, Peterborough, NH 03458. Reprinted by permission of Carus Publishing Company. **164.** "What Is Justice?" by Daniel Blanchard. Reprinted by permission. **173.** "The Road Not Taken" from *The Poetry of Robert Frost,* Henry Holt and Company, Inc., New York, 1916. Reprinted by permission of the publisher. **175.** "Hope Is the Thing with Feathers" by Emily Dickinson. Reprinted courtesy of Harvard University Press. **182.** "Taking the Plunge" by Matthew Root. Reprinted with permission. **185.** Statement of Purpose for graduate school essay by Hasan Halkali. Reprinted with permission.

Photo Credits